1492

1492

✦

THE FOURTH CARAVEL OF CHRISTOPHER COLUMBUS

Rita M. Stark

iUniverse, Inc.

New York Lincoln Shanghai

1492
THE FOURTH CARAVEL OF CHRISTOPHER COLUMBUS

iUniverse books may be ordered through booksellers or by contacting:

iUniverse
2021 Pine Lake Road, Suite 100
Lincoln, NE 68512
www.iuniverse.com
1-800-Authors (1-800-288-4677)

Because of the dynamic nature of the Internet, any Web addresses or links contained in this book may have changed since publication and may no longer be valid.

The views expressed in this work are solely those of the author and do not necessarily reflect the views of the publisher, and the publisher hereby disclaims any responsibility for them.

ISBN: 978-0-595-45702-1 (pbk)
ISBN: 978-0-595-70815-4 (cloth)
ISBN: 978-0-595-90003-9 (ebk)

Printed in the United States of America

Contents

List of Illustrations vii

Preface xiii

CHAPTER 1 Columbus' Secret 1

CHAPTER 2 King Ferdinand 1st and Queen Isabella 6

CHAPTER 3 The Reconquest of Granada 13

CHAPTER 4 The Expulsion of the Jews 18

CHAPTER 5 The Documents before the Departure 22

CHAPTER 6 The letter of Hernando de Talavera to Queen
Isabella 31

CHAPTER 7 The Ships 35

CHAPTER 8 The Crews 44

CHAPTER 9 Life aboard a Caravel 51

CHAPTER 10 The Instruments 55

CHAPTER 11 The Stop at Gomera 63

CHAPTER 12 The Letter to Santángel 69

CHAPTER 13 The Taíno Society 78

CHAPTER 14 The Return 89

CHAPTER 15 Annibale de Gennaro's Letter 93

CHAPTER 16 Pope Alexander VI's Bulls 97

Synopsis 105

Chronology 107
About the Author 109

List of Illustrations

Young Genovese 5

Doña Juana de Castile. 9

King Ferdinand 1st 10

Queen Isabella 11

Christopher Columbus. 12

Christopher Columbus in 1492 16

Seeking Royal Support 17

Regnu Hispaniae. 26

The world imagined in the 15th century. 27

Spain in the XV century. 27

Sketch of La Santa Maria 37

Sketch of La Pinta. 38

La Niña with lateen sails. 39

Sketch of La Niña 39

La Fusta used in the Mediterranean Sea 40

La Fusta used by Venetians 41

La Fusta in Santo Domingo. 42

Juan de la Cosa. 47

Martín Alonso Pinzón. 48

Vicente Yáñez Pinzón *49*

Sailor uniform *53*

Hour Glass *57*

The Cross-Staff *58*

Astrolabe used by Columbus *59*

Speed Calculator *60*

English Quadrant *61*

Compass rose *62*

Punta Salina *64*

Noticias de la Historia General de las Islas Canarias *66*

Doña Beatriz de Bobadilla Peraza *67*

First sighting of land *75*

Claiming a new world *76*

Historia Grafica de Española *81*

Columbus showing a Spanish coin to a Taíno *82*

Taíno pottery *83*

Taíno pottery *84*

Taíno conic dwelling *85*

Taíno divinity *86*

Columbus invoking blessing on Española *87*

Columbus welcomed at Barcelona *91*

Columbus presenting natives *91*

Reporting discoveries *92*

Pope Alexander VI *99*

Demarcation lines *100*

Columbus' coat of arms in Genoa. *101*

Columbus' coat of arms in Seville. *102*

Columbus' coat of arms in Palos. *103*

Monument in the garden of the Alcazar, Cordoba. *108*

Acknowledgments

Many thanks to Mr. Gary Herrick, The Computer Professor, for processing the illustrations.

Preface

Columbus achieved his discovery of America with not only three ships, but with four. This discovery is interesting because it reflects that history, like any other science, is not perfect. When the data to complete a study do not give us satisfactory answers, we must recur to a process of hypotheses, which is not contrary to history, but very often has no possibility of being verified. Due to the fact that this period is a key-time in world history, a study of the documents preceding the departure, as well as the ones after the return, becomes necessary to corroborate the presence of a fourth ship and not let the hypotheses become the principal element of our research.

In the year 1492 the most important enterprises requested by Spanish politics to be accomplished by the Catholic Kings were the following: the re-conquest of Granada and the expulsion of the Jews. In the discovery-conquest of the new routes to the Indies to colonize new lands, it was a political, social, economical, and psychological necessity to obtain recognition from the Pope, who was in charge of allotting these "nobody's lands" to bypass the various Catholic Kings, who all deferred to the Pope.

History and Experience.

"When events follow in chronological order, they evolve in affinity with the ones that have preceded them. They depend from one another, not always and exclusively out of necessity, but like a mesh well woven rationally." These words from Emperor Marcus Aurelius Antoninus taken from his book *"Meditations"* or *"Soliloquies"* indicate a method of understanding historic events by realizing an association between the time of our life and the historic time.

The past becomes an abstract category if we do not realize the connection with our experiences. So also past human activities can lose their meaning if we take them out of the longer historical context.

Often the experience, the direct acquaintance of the persons, and the knowledge of the motivations that have brought them to act in a certain manner require an objective understanding conditioned to the degree of intelligence, culture, and sensibility to study a certain historic period.

Very rarely two persons describe a witnessed event in the same manner. Each one records the part that has made an impression on his/her subconscious.

The XV century was a century of deep crisis in ideals. What characterizes a certain era can be discovered in a period of crisis when a choice has to be made. Old ideologies, lifestyles, and traditions are hard to kill while the newborn ideologies have not yet been able to impose themselves.

Another characteristic of crises is that they do not manifest themselves always in the same social class—an economic crisis hits always the poorest members of the population, but an intellectual crisis can manifest itself in two contradictory manners.

When an elite sets itself apart from the way the usual society is meant to be, it imposes a vision of life that is no longer real. Such an elite operates in a world completely separated from reality. This type of crisis is born each time a group of intellectuals generates ideas or actions to leave behind an imprint of power or superiority.

This phenomenon occurs each time a scientific discovery puts in jeopardy the belief of certain human or religious values considered unchangeable. The perfect example is Galileo, who challenged a millennia old belief.

It is certain, however, that no matter what the motivations or beliefs are, crises create a chain-reaction that involves the whole society. If this society is not able to react, it will be destroyed by the new forces that have emerged from the crisis and received confirmation through an entire intellectual revolution.

The element of time.

In the XV century the perception of time was completely different from the concept we have today. The Renaissance man accepted with enthusiasm everything that was attached to human experience, because it was supported by the intellect. It is the intellect that allows the individual to do "what he wants." It is in this *"Humanitas"* that the love for the Arts and the Letters reconcile with the practicality of the every day life, intended as experience. When we realize who we are, time acquires more value and we understand the importance of our actions.

Columbus' *"sensus sui"* (= conscience of himself) had already emerged when he began thinking to his voyage of discovery, but it took the superior intelligence of a ruler to realize the most appropriate political opportunity to bring it to completion.

The man of the XV century begins to realize the advantage in actions accomplished in a rational manner even if, some time, a wait longer than expected is required. When this happens a study of the past becomes useful in our every day lives to bring us into the future.

At this point we need to consider that Spain and Portugal were the two most apt nations on the Atlantic to sail toward a new world. From one of the two the idea to sail to the Indies was expected to be born. Every European nation was aware of this fact, because even the foreign ambassadors to the Spanish Court were proposing it. But we will explain later the reason why Spain was the nation capable of realizing this enterprise. Right now the most important factor to notice is the geographical location.

For Columbus, however, the most crucial factor was the discovery of a new *Habitat*, where new cities could be built because his purpose was colonization, not exploitation of a natural environment so hospitable.

1

Columbus' Secret

Since the age of nineteen, Columbus had navigated the waters of the Atlantic Ocean at the service of the King of Portugal. In 1481 he had started corresponding with an Italian astrologer, Paolo del Pozzo Toscanelli, who had drawn a very accurate world map indicating that the Indies could be reached not only by land, as Marco Polo had done, but also by crossing *"The Sea of Darkness."*

The astrologer sent his map with a letter to the King of Portugal's advisors and told Columbus. From the moment this information was received at court, Columbus tried numerous times to convince the king and his advisors to finance an expedition to *"buscar el Levante por el Poniente"* (= to seek the East via the West), but he was always rejected.

In 1484 something else happened that gave Columbus even more positive information about a world on the other side of the Atlantic Ocean. Alonso Sánchez de Huelva, a naval pilot also at the service of Portugal and Columbus' friend, while sailing between the Canary Islands and Madeira, was overtaken by a terrible storm that brought the ship about seven hundred and fifty leagues away from her destination to an island in the middle of the Atlantic Ocean (thought by many to be Bermuda). From there, while returning to Portugal with only five men left in the crew, Alonso landed in Terceira—an island in the Azores Archipelago belonging to Portugal and so called because it was the third to be discovered—where Columbus welcomed him in his home. Although some historians of the period did not accept this information because it was not exactly known whether Columbus lived in the island of Terceira, Gonzalo Fernández de Oviedo was the first author to write about this event in 1535.

He was Columbus and Vicente Pinzón's friend and went to the new world as inspector of mines. In his book *"Historia general y natural de las Indias, islas y tierra firme del Mar Océano"* he wrote the following:

"Some would have it that a caravel going to Spain from England happened to be driven by such strong winds that she was forced to sail toward the west for many days until were discovered one or more islands near the Indies. When the sailors went ashore, they saw the natives going about naked.... When the caravel started sailing toward the European coast, the winds were favorable and reached it in a very short time ... "

All men on board had died except the captain and three or four of them, who were extremely ill and died shortly after having come ashore. It is also said that the captain was Columbus' friend and he understood astrology. He had marked the outlines of a land he had found and, in great secrecy, had told Columbus about it. Columbus begged him to draw a map while he was resting in his house and being cared for his illness. He did but died shortly after of an unknown disease like the other sailors.

In this manner Columbus found out about the new discovered land in the middle of the Atlantic Ocean and had all the coordinates to enable him to reach it. However Columbus was alone when his friend died and there was no witness to corroborate his story. De Oviedo ended his narration with these words: *"In my opinion it is a falsehood."* But the historians of the era agreed upon the fact that, because the captain died in Columbus' home, all the papers of his ship must have been left there.

Bartolomé de Las Casas, who had witnessed in Barcelona Columbus' arrival from his voyage of discovery, in his book *"Historias de las Indias"* gives us many important details and states that: *"from that day on Columbus had the sure knowledge that, after navigating from the Island of Hierro in the Canary Islands, approximately seven hundred fifty leagues west of it, he would find land."* But he kept this information secret. The proof of this theory came during the second voyage when on November 3, 1493, exactly seven hundred and fifty leagues west of Hierro he found a small island, measuring twenty square kilometers, six leagues west of Guadalupe in the French Antilles.

Some of the natives reported that Columbus had named this island *"La Desecada"* because he found it very arid and depressing. But De Oviedo and Santa Cruz gave another explanation: *"The first land he found and discovered was an island which, as soon as he saw it, he named "Deseada" because of the desire he and his crew had to see land."*

Apparently the story told by the natives did not seem to be supported by any documents, while the old maps have always shown the Spanish name *"La Deseada"* and the Portuguese *"La Desejada"*—the two words meaning the same thing. But it is true that Columbus wanted to keep the discovery of this island a secret because there is no mention of it in *"The Log"* and moreover, Michele da Cuneo, a reporter from Savona, Italy, friend of Columbus' family, who took part in the expedition, described with great emphasis only the discovery of the other islands—Dominica, Maria Galante, and Guadalupe in his *"Relazione"* to Messer Gerolamo Annari.

Manzano in his book *"Colón descubrió America del Sur en 1494"* calls Columbus *"the sole beneficiary of the great secret of the unknown pilot"* adding furthermore *"Columbus deprived his friend of the glory of this great discovery"* implying that he used the information for his own advantage.

The fact is that by the end of 1484 Columbus had in his possession very valuable documents—the letters and the map of Toscanelli and the charts of the dead friend. This was all the evidence he needed to locate land on the other side of the Atlantic Ocean.

After the death of his wife and the continuous rejections of the King of Portugal, he decided to move to Castile with his son Diego and offer his services to the Spanish Crown.

While in Spain he learned that his exploration rivals, the brothers Pinzón, were in possession of a map drawn by Esdras, a cartographer of the period, and were also considering an expedition of discovery. However, Toscanelli's map was much more accurate and scientific. The only problem was that Columbus could not divulge to the Spanish Monarchs Toscanelli's letters and map because they had been expressly prepared for the Portuguese court. He had to find a way to send the information secretly. He wrote to Friar Juan Pérez about his being in possession of a very important document and asked him to reveal it secretly to the Spanish Monarchs.

Salvador de Madariaga, Spanish diplomat, writer, and historian of liberal tendencies, was communicating with several European Embassies, and wrote to them: *"Obviously the letter Friar Pérez wrote to the Catholic Kings had revealed a new fact, important enough to change the course of events. Also the queen thought that it would be best to discuss in private with Friar Pérez this revelation before calling Columbus. In fact the revelation of Friar Pérez was of such nature that it settled once and for all the cosmographical aspect of Columbus' plan."*

The Spanish Monarchs received Columbus at court in January of 1486 and allowed him to submit his expedition's plan of discovery. A commission of experts nominated by the Crown met in Salamanca and Cordova to examine Columbus' plans. The verdict, however, was negative because the war against the

Moors was still going on and depleting the treasury. The queen advised Columbus to resubmit the project to the commission at a later time.

In 1488 at his return from Portugal Columbus had met Antonio Giraldini
and they had become very good friends. On his deathbed Antonio had recom-
mended Columbus to his brother Alejandro encouraging him to help the Genovese. The friendship between the Admiral and Alejandro became so great that
Columbus named the discovered island of Berequeya "*Graciosa*" after his friend's
mother.

Alejandro and Pedro de Mendoza, who as third party mediated the dispute
between Castile and Aragon in favor of Columbus, convinced the queen completely of the navigator's genius.

Young Genovese working for Portugal.
Oil on canvas by artist Juan Medina Ramirez,
Santo Domingo.

2

King Ferdinand 1st and Queen Isabella

Legend has credited Queen Isabella with the financial support needed for the greatest discovery of the century, but historians have disagreed whether the credit should be given exclusively to the queen or should be shared with her husband. It is sure, however, that, right after the refusal of the commission of experts in 1486, Queen Isabella met Columbus in Jaén and gave him hope that she would consider again his request as soon as circumstances would permit. She asked Columbus to remain in Spain at the expenses of the Crown and supported his ideas while waiting for the war against the Moors to conclude.

From the *"Noticias Legalizadas de las Erogaciones de la Corona"* (= Legal notices of distributions from the Crown) we know that, between May 5, 1487 and August 3, 1492, the time of departure for the first voyage, Columbus was being regularly paid in *maravedís*. On May 5, 1487 he received 3,000 *maravedís* by decree of Alonso de Quintanilla upon mandate of the Bishop of Palencia for accomplishing special tasks at the service of Their Highnesses. On August 27 of the same year the Admiral received 4,000 *maravedís* by mandate of Their Highnesses and decree of the same bishop to defray the costs of a special departure on July 3, 4,000 more for another departure on October 15, and finally a last disbursement of 4,000 *maravedís* on June 16, 1488 by decree of Their Highnesses. In 1491 the accounting ledger of Luis de Santángel and Francisco Pinelo, Treasurers of the Fraternity, showed that Columbus had received a total sum of 140,000 *maravedís*. This same entry appears in the accounting ledger of García Martínez and Pedro de Montemayor in the year 1492 where was also specified the reason why—*"to pay for the caravels that Their Highnesses are sending as fleet to the Indies and to pay for Columbus who goes with the fleet."*

Queen Isabella kept her promises. She was a strong and loving woman and she admired Columbus' pride and genius. Even though she and the navigator were of the same age and temperament, she never loved him. All through her life she did not know any other love than Ferdinand's. She had known times of hardship before becoming queen and she grew to be very intelligent, serious, honest, and pious. She used her intelligence to help her husband to create one of the greatest kingdoms in Europe.

Her ascent to the throne of Castile had not been without lack of opposition. She owed the crown to the turbulent nobility of the kingdom who forced her brother and predecessor, Enrique IV, to resign and proclaim her sister Queen of Castile. Further more Enrique IV had to take away from his own daughter, Juana, all rights of succession.

Not less full of grave events were the circumstances that brought Ferdinand to the throne of Aragon. He was the son of King Juan II and his second wife, Juana Enriquez of Castile. Carlos de Viana, first son of King Juan II, and his first wife Bianca of Navarre were the rightful heirs to the throne of Aragon. Upon the death of Bianca, however, because her will did not specify the power between the surviving husband and her son heir, a long time of conflict had started. Carlos, nevertheless, had been recognized as the Lieutenant General of Navarre but the two countries had become opposite factions.

The nobility of the plains supported Juan II in wanting Ferdinand to become king; the nobility of the mountains supported Carlos. After many years of battles King Juan II acknowledged Carlos' birthright and promised him the throne and the marriage to Isabella. But Carlos died suddenly and suspicion arose about him being poisoned by his stepmother, Juana Enriquez. Now Ferdinand was left the sole heir to the throne of Aragon and was recognized as such by the *Cortés* of Catalayud in 1461 and he became King of Aragon in 1479 at Juan II's death.

At the same time in Castile, Juana, daughter of Enrique IV, who had been dispossessed of her rights of succession, had gathered many nobles, including the King of Portugal, to bring war to Isabella. This civil war ended in 1479 and it was time for Isabella to marry Ferdinand, who was substituting his dead brother in uniting the two Houses.

The nobility was against this substitution, therefore, the new reign began during very unfavorable times in the midst of hostilities. The new monarchs had to rule strongly and at the same time tactfully and diplomatically. The use of special concessions to gain favors from the nobility had to be abolished due to the fact that this particular behavior had already caused the last civil war in Spain.

It was not by chance that, when Ferdinand and Isabella became King and Queen of Castile and Aragon, they decided to restart the war against the Moors.

Machiavelli wrote in *"The Prince"* about the Spanish Monarchs and their Holy Wars: *"... it lasted a long time because of the difficulties of the situation and also because Ferdinand wanted to weaken the military strength of the nobility by keeping its soldiers occupied in the re-conquest of the Spanish territories to unite Spain and make them feel part of a military campaign led by the king himself."*

At the end of the year 1491 the re-conquest of Granada was bringing to an end the unification of Spain. But the Catholic Monarchs were not ready to stop here. They had two other projects to accomplish in 1492: the expulsion of the Jews to bring them revenues from what they were forced to leave behind and Columbus' enterprise to solve the problems of the nobility by conveying its interests toward new rich lands to exploits.

Portrait of Doña Juana I of Castile.
Museo de Las Casas Reales, Santo Domingo.

Portrait of King Ferdinand 1st.
Casa de Colón, Las Palmas, Grand Canary.

Portrait of Queen Isabella.
Casa de Colón, Las Palmas, Grand Canary.

Portrait of Columbus.
Casa de Colón, Las Palmas, Grand Canary.

3

The Reconquest of Granada

At the beginning of the VIII century the Muslims invaders from North Africa began the conquest of Southern Spain and took at least three fourths of the peninsula. By the X century the Caliphate of Cordoba was a very sophisticated Arab Empire that left a visible mark on the country. A small minority of Jews managed to survive under Muslim rule by remaining neutral while Spain began a campaign of re-conquest of the lost territories.

Ferdinand III and Alfonso X regained the valley of the Guadalquivir and Murcia leaving the Muslim Spain very reduced in power as well as in territory. The successor of Alfonso X, Alfonso XI, defeated definitively the Muslims in the battle of the Salado River in 1340 and took back the Fortress of Gibraltar ending this way the danger of new African invasions. The only territory left to the Muslims—of what was called Al-Andalus—was the reign of Granada, where Mohammed Ibn Nasr consolidated a dynasty that lasted until the Catholic Monarchs began their campaign of re-conquest (1481-1492) to unify Spain.

When in 1482 the Spanish *Cortés* gave their consent to a definitive final campaign against the kingdom of the Moors, Pope Sixtus IV acknowledged with a Papal Bull this enterprise as a crusade and sent as an appeal to the Christians of France, England, Germany, Switzerland, and even Poland to unite with the Spaniards "... *who were committed to re-conquer Granada and every meter of Spanish territory still under the domination of the Infidel.*"

The King Moor in vain asked for help from the Sultan of Constantinople, Bayazid II, who limited himself to complain to the pontiff about the cruelties and the violent pillages the Spaniards were inflicting on the Muslims in the cities they had conquered and threatened to retaliate on the Christians living in his Sultanate.

Ferdinand and Isabella answered the pope that the territories occupied by the Moors were property of their ancestors and the King of Granada had no legal jurisdiction over them. The Spanish Sovereigns were simply defending the Christians living in these territories; therefore this war was becoming a legitimate defense of Christianity. The retaliations of Sultan Bayazid II in the Orient were no concern of Spain.

In 1483 another Moorish king was reigning: Boabdil I. He had been captured by the Spaniards but released under the following conditions:

1. He had to declare himself a subject of the Kingdom of Castile.

2. He had to pay a tribute of 12,000 gold doubloons.

3. He had to free 400 Christian prisoners.

4. He had to allow free transit to the Christian army through his territory.

5. He had to promise to appear at court each time he was summoned.

6. He had to send his son as hostage to some members of the Spanish nobility.

7. He had to respect a truce of two years.

But King Boabdil did not respect the last condition of the treaty and declared the "*Holy War*" on Spain. King Boabdil was defeated; the city of Granada capitulated on November 25, 1491 and was handed over to the Spanish Monarchs within sixty-five days from the capitulation.

On January 2, 1492, two hours before daylight, the two most important dignitaries of the province came to the city with horses and infantry. A Moor named Monier and another named Alben Maiar showed the Spanish dignitaries some secret passages to the Alhambra trough back streets. Then Monier opened the main gates and let the Spanish soldiers in. Boabdil left the fortress with a garrison of 600 soldiers. He rode to the mountainside of his beloved city to take the last view of it and bid farewell with a great sigh. The location where he turned his horse around to leave Spain forever became known as "*El ultimo suspiro del Moro.*" (= The Moor's last sigh).

The Christian army, after having taken possession of the palace, erected an altar and celebrated Mass. They also raised a huge cross on the highest tower of the city and everybody acclaimed. Among the acclaiming crowd there was also Columbus, who now felt that it was the right time to reinforce his requested support for the discovery of the new lands to import spices and gold to refurbish the Royal Treasury.

This conquest completely satisfied the emotions and the fantasy of the XV century man, who had lived for many years preoccupied with the presence of the

Infidel in his land. With the conquest of Granada and the unification of Spain, Isabella and Ferdinand had acquired great prestige in the eyes of the world and had been recognized officially as "*The Catholic Kings.*"

They wanted to maintain this image and were beginning to plan a crusade to help the Italians with their problems with the Turks, who still possessed Otranto on the Adriatic Sea. Columbus was very aware of that; therefore he began to emphasize religion and colonization to make them play an important role in this voyage of discovery. He wrote a letter to King Ferdinand stating: "*I declare to Their Highnesses that all the income generated by my enterprise can be spent to conquer the Infidel.*"

Columbus in 1492.
Courtesy of the Christopher Columbus Philatelic Society.

Courtesy of the Christopher Columbus Philatelic Society.

4

The Expulsion of the Jews

Toward the end of the XV century the word "*Infidel*" was not describing only the Moors and the Muslims but also anyone of another religion opposing Christianity. These persons did not have any civil rights. Special privileges—beside the ones offered by the common laws—could be given to them by private civic communities but revocable at any time without a plausible explanations.

Just to give an example, a Spanish Jew was simply a Jew born in Spain by chance. He had nothing in common with his compatriots. Relations between Jews and Christians were limited by the Christian canon laws and kept to a minimum or forbidden altogether. The many voices raised in favor of religious tolerance were never heard.

Only the "*Infidel*" who had been converted to Christianity could enjoy all the civil rights of a Christian community. The Jews were tolerated: the sporadic periods of persecution were based on events like epidemics, famine, earthquakes, and flood believed to be a divine punishment for a society admitting the presence of non-believers.

These specific situations offered people the opportunity to rob the ghettoes, kill, and loot the members of the Jewish community. Such riots happened against the will of the authorities and, particularly in Spain, against the will of the monarchs, who had adopted pro-Semitic political policies.

But during the second half of the XV century a new slow change in politics occurred with the birth of the National States. They characteristically centralized the power in the hands of the rulers thereby making all laws equal for everyone in the territory. They also took away from the nobility all privileges and invited them to court to control them better and reduce cause for rebellion.

As the monarchy became more and more consolidated, it enforced the religious observances and the cults were suppressed. It became apparent that a plausible pretext to eliminate these contrary forces within the nation needed to be found.

Religious unity brought spiritual consolidation in Spain. Also the possibility of taking all the Jewish community's riches accumulated during centuries and the non-restitution of loans, made to the Crown during the war against the Moors, became the main reason for the monarchs to become malevolent toward the Jews. In fact the Jewish community could enjoy religious freedom—due to their enormous economic prosperity—while the members of the lower Spanish classes, who had not been able to accumulate wealth, envied them.

The Jews were also practicing usury, which was prohibited by Christian laws because the earnings from lending money were calculated by the time of the loan and time was considered to be a gift of God and not human possession. Usury so involved a speculation on something that did not belong to man. Nevertheless usury remained a monopoly of the Jews for a century and the term *"Jew"* became synonymous with a person who lends money at a high rate of interest, not just a believer of another faith.

Another monopoly of the Spanish Jews was the administration of the crown's fiscal department. This fact made them even more hated by the people because they were in charge of collecting taxes, even to the point of using force.

The Christian population, being superior in number and convinced of their religion's transcendence, knew that the Jews, even if converted, would never be completely assimilated. So the *"Edict of Expulsion"* was presented as an act of thankfulness to God for making Spain victorious over another crusade against the *"Infidel."*

Even though the regions of Castile and Aragon kept their own autonomous laws after Isabella's marriage to Ferdinand, the tribunal of the Inquisition was a powerful weapon over all of Spain. This religious instrument had already unified Spain even before the real union took place and its goal was to attack the Jews who would not convert. So the Jews had to practice in secret their religion while, on the other hand, give the impression of complying with the religious practices requested by a Christian society.

The processes of the Inquisition, which had originally started exclusively against the Jews, began to include everyone who was not Catholic. Whoever did not want to convert was considered an offender of the clergy and therefore accused of heresy. It is believed that the idea of a mass expulsion of the Jews had originated during the time when Tomás de Torquemada was Great Inquisitor.

The monarchs, however, considered the re-conquest of Granada more important and they borrowed from Jews huge sums of money for this endeavor. At the same time the Jewish community felt that, by helping Spain in this religious war, could be better accepted in Spanish society. But it was not so.

The richest Israelite, Don Isaac Abrabanel, had been charged with pleading this cause by introducing the most cultured church doctors and rabbis to formulate an exposé of Jewish history in Spain during the past century. But in doing this they were not realizing that, even if born in Spain, they were still considering themselves guests and foreigners in a nation that in reality was their homeland. In fact their strict belief in maintaining the traditions of their ancestors kept them in Spanish society's margins.

So on March 31, 1492 the *"Edict of Expulsion'* was officially announced all over Spain. Even though its context was based on the idea of uniting Spain through religion, this mass expulsion brought immense financial gains and more prestige to the monarchs to be called *"Defensores Fidei"* (=Defenders of the Faith).

However this new title for the Catholic Monarchs would not be acknowledged in other European nations. When Pope Alexander VI's Bull assigned to Ferdinand and Isabella jurisdiction over the lands in the New World, this decision was not based on the expulsion of the Jews but solely on the re-conquest of Granada. The evicted, in fact, sought protection from the Vatican and the pope placed them in Italian territories belonging to the Church known as the Pontifical States. The edict was also valid in Sardinia, Sicily, and the Kingdom of Naples, which were possessions of Spain ruled by Ferdinand's brother, Don Ferrante King of Naples and of the Two Sicilies.

It is not certain how much monetary gain this expulsion brought to the Spanish Crown, but according to information based on data provided by Abrabanel and Abraham Senior—Comptrollers General of Taxation—more than three hundred thousand families had to sell their possessions at extremely low prices because they were not allowed to take with them anything more than the bare necessities. The deadline for this evacuation was set for July 31, 1492 but later was changed to August 2 for political reasons and to avoid too much publicity on Columbus' voyage.

Already the repercussions of the Inquisition as well as the disappearance of the Arab culture in Spain generated an internal social division. The Arabs were masters in Science and Medicine, disciplines very much in demand all over the known world and only available in Spain: therefore Spain lost all the possible contacts depending on them. Once the Jews had left, on one side there was the rich nobility and on the other the increasing poverty in the lower classes because of the lack of the kind of bourgeoisie with spirit of initiative and commercialism that was able to meet the requirements of both classes.

The mercantile future of Spain was based on the Jews, who had created a commercial bourgeoisie capable of supporting the nation's economy. The nobility, used to luxury and idleness interrupted only by military campaigns, was not able to play such role. Columbus' enterprise was fulfilling the dreams of the poor as well as the nobility in discovering a new world that could be exploited. But at this time, not knowing what the new lands could offer in terms of colonization, everyone's goal was strictly to import slaves, spices, and gold with the hope that this great enterprise could bring a better plan of colonization in the future.

5

The Documents before the Departure

After the Spanish victory over the Moors, Queen Isabella sent Columbus 20,000 maravedís *"to buy decent clothes to go on a visit to their Highnesses"* and invited him to court. The queen's special invitation and the extra amount of money made Columbus realize that the Sovereigns were ready to take action.

Upon suggestion of Marchena and Antonio Geraldini, who were the Papal ambassadors in Spain during the time of the re-conquest of Granada, the queen submitted Columbus' plans to a Commission of Grandees instead of scientists and theologians. The idea was finally accepted for three positive reasons.

Firstly the expedition's cost was not very high. Secondly the risk of compromising lives was also low so, in case of deaths among the members of the crew, the Sovereigns would not be criticized too severely. Thirdly, in case of success, the advantages would be enormous for the economy and the international politics of the nation. The discovery of new routes to the Indies was going to enhance even more the Spanish Crown's prestige across Europe and, internally, to unite under the same crown those citizens who were still unassimilated.

Furthermore the city of Palos had been sentenced to equip the Monarchs' two caravels with arms and supplies for a year's term because its citizens had committed infractions against them. The remainder of the money and goods had to be provided by the Councilors and local bankers. The Monarchs were also considering using the same forces the nobility had provided for the re-conquest of Granada so they would not remain idle.

In such a light the discovery of America seemed to be a very well calculated risk instead of a dream. Also Columbus had at court many *"protectors"*—as he used to call his supporters. The most important among them was Luis de Santángel who was *"Escribano de ración"* (position similar to Minister of Finances), Friar Juan Pérez, Friar Diego Deza, the Duke of Medinaceli, Alonso de Quintanilla,

Francesco Pinelli and other Italian bankers to whom the Sovereigns had been indebted for a long time. But at this time the financial situation had largely improved because of the massive expropriation of the Jews' assets and the advantages received from the re-conquest of Granada. By June 1492 it had been agreed to finance Columbus' expedition for the sum of 200,000,000 maravedís as long as the navigator's interests would coincide with the ones of the Crown.

Two very important documents indicate the official beginning of Columbus' expedition: *"Las Capitulaciónes de Santa Fé de la Vega de Granada (April 17, 1492) y La Cédula Real (April 30, 1492)"* plus four *"Provisiones"* (=ordinances) and one Decree. Les Capitulaciónes are so called because, during the time when King Ferdinand was in Granada fighting the King Moor, he had ordered the construction of a citadel within the walls of Granada called Santa Fé after a fire had destroyed the Christian camp. Before the re-conquest of this city Columbus had met here with the king and many other important personalities, who were forming a commission presided by Friar Hernando de Talavera and comprising Rodrigo Maldonado, Rodrigo de Alcocer, Mendoza and Giraldini. Juan Manzano, a specialist in the study of the Admiral's personality, writes: *"Probably Mendoza and Giraldini were the most ardent defenders of the Admiral's cause in Santa Fé."* The proposal was voted down because the commission thought that Columbus did not have enough experience.

The theologians, who had studied Columbus' plan, had judged him a heretic because Bishop Nicolás de Lira believed that the Orient ended at the Fortuna Islands and St. Augustine that the Antipodes did not exist. Columbus, then, decided to submit his plan to the King of France.

Queen Isabella, who was defending his cause but could not go against the majority of the vote, was exalted by Columbus with these words to Prince Juan: *"Everyone is a disbeliever, while our Lord has given to the Queen, our lady, spirit, intelligence, and great power; and I am telling you that she is for me a dear and much beloved daughter. The ignorance of all others transforms knowledge into an inconvenient fable."*

This citation and the fact that Columbus wanted to present his project to the Court of France was very favorable to Queen Isabella during the third meeting in Santa Fé, which made the commission finally decide upon the fact that Columbus should still remain in Spain. To the Archbishop of Seville, Diego Deza, the Archbishop of Granada, Friar Hernando de Talavera, and Cabrero, is due the triumph of the Admiral. But Luis de Santángel was the one who urged Queen Isabella to support Columbus' brilliant scientific arguments and so Columbus returned to Santa Fé after he had received letters from her.

Don Juan de Coloma was the Registrar of all the documents. Manzano writes: *"Luis de Santángel convinced the queen; Friar Diego Deza and Cabrero convinced the king."*

So with the documents written between King Ferdinand 1st and Columbus began the "Spanish-Columbian Period" in the history of Spain.

"Las Capitulaciónes de Santa Fé" is an instrument of capitulations written in Santa Fé de Granada on the 17th of April 1492 between the Catholic Monarchs and Christopher Columbus containing four paragraphs. The first paragraph states that the Monarchs authorize Columbus to sail the Ocean Sea to discover new lands making him the Admiral of the fleet with all the prerogatives that pertain to this office. The second paragraph states that Columbus will become Viceroy and Governor of all the lands discovered. The third paragraph states that Columbus will receive one tenth of all merchandise (meaning gold, spices, precious stones, etc.) discovered in the new lands. The fourth paragraph states that, in case of litigations with other merchants interested in the export of the same merchandise, it is the duty of the Admiral or his Lieutenant to mediate these litigations. Finally, if the Admiral wishes it, he can pay one eighth of the outfitting of the ships and be rewarded with one eighth of the profit.

The second document called *"Cédula Real"* is a royal license written on the 30th of April 1492 to give confirmation of everything stipulated in the *Capitulaciónes* besides giving Columbus the title of Captain of La Santa Maria, which was not a caravel but a *"nao"* making of this ship *"La Nao Capitana."* Once this license had been stipulated, Columbus was becoming Admiral and responsible for the other ships in the fleet. In this document it is the first time that are mentioned the words *"certain fustas"* in a very generic sense because such ships were owned by privateers, who wanted to follow Columbus of their own free will. They did not have anything to do with the expedition, whose main aspect was to emphasize the Christian mission of the Catholic Kings and Columbus had to obey and respect them *"as Captain General of Their Highnesses."*

On that same day—30th of April 1492—were also written five *"Provisiones"* (=ordinances). The first was specifying that the titles given to Columbus could be hereditary and therefore pass on to his successors. Up to this time Columbus had worked for Portugal and Spain as another crewmember, therefore he did not have any kind of title. However, because of the fact that he was very talented in calculus and geography, he was able to use those sciences to become a good cartographer. The other three, also written on the 30th of April 1492, were directed to the Citizens of Palos. The citizens of this city had committed infractions towards the

Monarchs and the Royal Council had condemned them to serve for two months and outfit at their own expenses two caravels and have them ready for Columbus' day of departure. They had also to provide tradesmen, food and kegs of water needed for the crossing. The two caravels equipped were La Pinta and La Niña. Once the two caravels had been equipped, the Monarchs issued a last ordinance for the citizens of Palos that stated that all jailed criminals were being pardoned and given their freedom if they would become member of the crews going to discover new lands. Not many took advantage of this opportunity basically because of superstition. As we will see in the letter written by Hernando the Talavera to Queen Isabella, sailing the Dark Sea and passing the Hercules' Columns (= the strait of Gibraltar) was a serious sin.

The last document was an edict about the elimination of taxes for every citizen in the whole Spain who had helped personally Columbus in outfitting "*the fustas*" that he was taking with him in this voyage of discovery. In this document the King does not mention the word "*Caravel*" but "*Fusta.*"

Emblem of Spain.

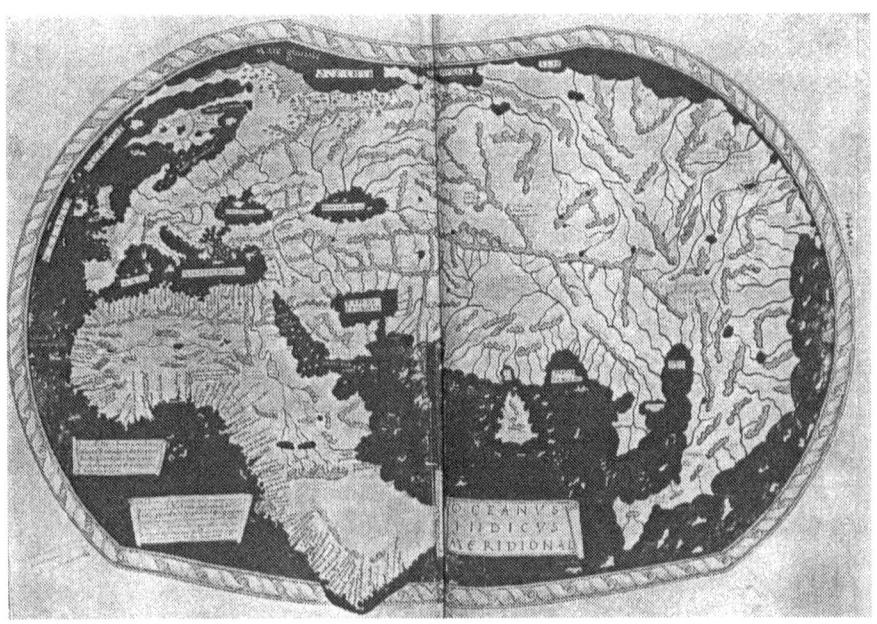

Planisphere designed by Enrico Martello circa 1483.
Panel at Casa de Colón, Grand Canary.

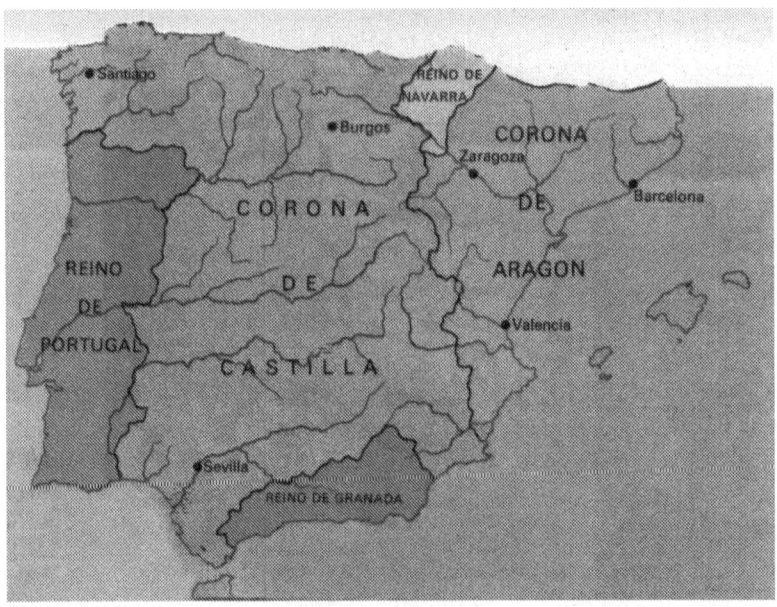

Spain in the XV century.

In 1935 Emiliano Jos discovered three other documents that proved that Columbus intended to cross the Atlantic Ocean to reach Asia, the Indies, Cathay, and Cipango. The first, dated 5th of May 1492 and found in the archives of Simancas, is the registration of a payment in the amount of 200,000 maravedís made to Louis de Santángel by Alonso de la Cabezas *"on account toward the sum of 400,000 maravedís needed by the king to equip the caravels sent to the Indies and to pay for Christopher Columbus, who sails with the aforesaid fleet."*

The second document is the *Passport,* a letter issued by the Catholic Monarchs addressed to all the rulers, first born sons and relatives of kings, dukes, marquis, captains, ship owners, officers and subjects, so that they shall facilitate in every manner Columbus' voyage. The *Passport* was also signed in Granada on the 17th of April 1492 and said: *"With this letter we send the nobleman Christopher Columbus with three caravels, outfitted for the Ocean Sea, toward the regions of India for certain reasons and affairs concerning the propagation of the divine faith and also for our own interests and benefits …"* Then the letter continue requesting from its recipients to receive well the Spanish delegation and allow free transit to *"… the noblemen, who are arriving with the caravels and other maritime vessels (vasa maritima) …"*

During the XV century the expression *"vasa maritima"* was a generalization indicating any type of maritime vessels. It did not mean that Columbus left with a fleet larger than he was able to equip, but it could be interpreted as an allusion to the fact that the three caravels constituted the basic ships needed for the expedition. The caravel was the most outstanding type of ship at this time to sustain an oceanic voyage. The manner in which maritime vessels were described was very vague, unless detailed information was given for specific reasons. Therefore the emphasis was put on the caravels because she was a very specific and special kind of vessel.

The third document—like the *Passport*—was also found in the General Archives of the Crown of Aragon in Barcelona and it is a letter of introduction from the Spanish Sovereigns to the ruler of Cathay. However the name of the addressee is left out because the Spanish Monarchs did not know the name of the Grand Khan's successor, who was not the ruler at the time of Marco Polo. The fleet Notary, Rodrigo de Escobedo, was in charge of filling in the blanks upon arrival. This letter was also dated the 30th of April 1492 in Granada in triplicates and in Latin as a form of respect. In an era when the Spanish language was evolving and becoming more modern and popular, Latin was considered the language of scholars affiliated with the Church and City Officials. At any court there were plenty of men who knew Latin and could translate very easily any kind of communication written in this language. So the Spanish Monarchs considered normal policy to write to the ruler of Cathay, or the Emperor of Japan, or any other potentate encountered during the expedition, in the language known in all the courts.

Letter of Introduction.

"To the most serene Prince, our dearest friend:
We Ferdinand and Isabella, King and Queen of Castile, Aragon, Leon, Sicily, Granada, etc. send greetings and best wishes of prosperity. We know from our subjects and from others who have come here from other realms, what good will and what excellent consideration You show toward us and our state and Your great desire to be informed of our happenings. We have, therefore, resolved to send to You our noble Captain Christopher Columbus, bearer of this letter from which You can learn of our good health and fortune and other things that we have ordered him to tell You from us. We beg You, therefore, to have no doubts about what he will tell You on our behalf. As far as us, we would be most happy to show how ready we are to grant You wishes."

I THE KING—I THE QUEEN

"From our city in Granada, 30 April 1492, in three copies.
Secretary: Juan de Coloma."

BIBLIOGRAPHY

FCO. José Arnaíz, S.J.: *"Mas Luces que Sombras."* Chapter 7, p.55. Editora Amigo del Hogar, August 1989, Santo Domingo, Republica Dominicana.

Alejandro Geraldini: *"Cristobál Colón: Siete Años Decisivos de su Vida"* **(1485-1492)** pp.315-322. Editora Arzobispado de Santo Domingo, 1987.

Juan Peréz de Tudela: *"Revista de Indias."* Istituto Gonzalo Fernandez de Oviedo. Consejo superior de Investigaciónes Cientificas. Year 13, No. 54, October-December 1953 pp. 609-610.

Navarrete I, document V, pp. 302-303.

Navarrete I, document VI, pp. 304-305.

Navarrete I, document VII, pp.305-307.

Navarrete I, document VIII, p. 307.

Navarrete I, document IX, pp. 307-308.

Navarrete I, document X, pp. 308-309

Paolo Emilio Taviani: *"The Great Design."* Pp. 394-395. Instituto Geografico de Agostini, 1992, Novara, Italy.

Marinella Bonvini Mazzanti: *"1492, Scoperta e Conquista dell'America."* Pp. 102-103. Studi Storici Universitá di Urbino, Italy.

Rosa Ortega Canodell: Area de Ciencias Sociales, Orbe Pais, Historia. P. 251.

Primo Magazine: Issue Nov.-Dec. 2005 from National Italian-American Foundation, Washington D.C.

6

The letter of Hernando de Talavera to Queen Isabella

Even though Hernando de Talavera had been part of the commission agreeing on Columbus remaining in Spain during the first part of the year 1492, once all the legalities had been concluded with the registration of the documents signed between Columbus and the Monarchs by the 30th of April 1492, he tried to convince Queen Isabella not to support Columbus in this voyage of discovery. He sent her the following letter during the month of June of the same year:

"To her Highness, Queen Isabella, Sovereign by supreme grace, Queen of Castile, Léon, Toledo, Murcia, etc.

My fervent worry for the salvation of Your Highness' eternal soul incites me to address to you these lines dictated by the circumstances, in great haste and not appropriate for your august position. Please, pardon the fear and the sincere solicitude that I have for my queen. Here are the words that I address to my clement monarch.

My friend, Alonso de Quintanilla, has advised me of Your Highness' decision of giving royal support and generous aid to this "foreigner" called Christopher Columbus to sail on his ships toward the outer occidental sea, that, as of today, nobody has dared to sail. I have been told that by going toward the West this Columbus expects to reach the faraway realm of the Infidel—in other words the realms of China and the Indies.

Through these poor lines my wish is to beseech Your Highness, for the salvation of her immortal soul, to renounce to this foolish enterprise inspired to this stranger by Satan himself. It is not without reason that God, Master of the Universe and our Father Savior, has put to the entrance to the outer sea at the occidental boundary of the great and powerful realm of Your Highness, the two rocks called by the ancient Greeks "The Columns of Hercules."

Our Lord has put those two terrible rocks in the waves of the sea to advise his creatures that here is the limit of their expansion. Never human beings departed on ships in such direction have returned safe. This fact is the proof that this frontier has been banished for us mortals by our eternal Father. Whoever has the insolence of passing this line established by the Master of the universe violates in his foolishness the divine laws and puts his soul in danger for eternity in the same manner as the persons who are aiding him to revolt against God's will.

Your Highness should understand that, as Confessor of my august queen, I have the mission on this earth of protecting scrupulously the salvation of her soul; therefore I cannot remain silent in seeing the disaster that menaces it.

I implore my Queen to listen to me: it is not my modest person or my indignant language that speaks to your ears, Your Highness, but the Holy Fathers of the Church, who want to protect the souls of the faithful. If it were the will of the Holy Trinity to see its sons depart toward the outer seas, would our God have waited for the arrival of an "anonymous foreigner" whose origins are not known to anyone?

In the same manner that our Lord Jesus Christ inspired his emissary Saint Paul to go on our great sea (the Mediterranean) to bring the good news to the Greek Isles, Athens, Rome, and many other lands, He would have asked him to cross the outer ocean for the same saint mission if it had been his will. In his divine reason He knew that no mortal would be able to surpass the limit that God had already established for the faithful. Whoever goes over those limits sins and loses his soul for eternity.

If Your Highness, my august Queen, would allow it, I shall pass from religious affairs—that should not be expressed by my modest person but by the angels charged of this salvation to make him aware of the divine commandments—with your graceful permission to profane affairs and ask which kind of utility will come for Your Majesty from the voyage of this mentioned Columbus.

If his ships sink to the bottom of the sea—thing that these sinners deserve—he would unfortunately realize how deadly is this project. But if he returns from this infamous realm of the Orient with a heavy cargo of gold and precious stones, we cannot imagine the amplitude of the disaster that will hit our unfortunate country, because all young men of valor will imitate this sinner Columbus and abandon their wives and the young boys will abandon their fiancées to depart for the West.

Spain will lose her best sons, the women will feel abandoned, the children will feel orphans, and the fields deserted, our churches empty, our boundaries left open to enemies, who will be able to attack us without obstacles. If it is true that our Savior has allowed to our august Queen and the King her spouse to be victorious, after plenty of effort, over our false prophet Mohammed, and purify in this manner their kingdom from the Infidel, Mohammed's followers, who have not perish, will assemble on the outer ocean with the intention of taking revenge on Spain.

Emissaries will sail on rapid ships on the routes going from the proud and cruel King of the Moors to the greatest king of the Infidel, who, in the past, conquered and reduced the Saint City of Constantinople to ask for mercy because he wanted to make it the capital of his impure empire. He had vision of war to re-conquer Spain that was his property during the past centuries. How will we resist such an enemy so thirsty for revenge if our men will be on the outer sea after having left our land without defense? I wish I were wrong, but it can be the Heaven's punishment if we dare to defy the divine commandments in going over the limits already established. I think that even the great merit due to Your Majesty for having freed our holy land, with God's help, of the other Infidels—the ones who have nailed Christ our Savior to the cross, the traitor Jews—will not suffice to save your soul.

There is worse and I am trembling. My conscience forces me to scare your royal ears with the terrible and deadly news that I have just received. In my sadness I am foreseeing the disaster reserved for you and this sinner Columbus. I have gone in pilgrimage to Friar Juan, who lives as a hermit in the mountains above Granada always covered with snow. Your Highness must have heard of Friar Juan, who for 40 years has not eaten much, does not bathe or shave. I went to visit him to make him aware of the great disgrace menacing us.

While we were talking, bitter tears came out of his eyes. Shaken, this holy man asked how "the evil one" was able to make such a criminal enter the heart of Your Highness. As soon as the emotions left him, he asked me to aid him in prayer with the purpose of avoiding disaster. We have prayed all night until dawn, and then we fell asleep.

Once we woke up, Friar Juan told me of the nightmare he had. In this dream appeared to him one of Our Lord's envoy, Saint John the Baptist, who informed him that if Spain sins against God, if her ships cross the frontiers not allowed to be crossed by mortals, we will lose all hope to free some day the Holy Land from the Infidel. And not only the Infidel will continue to dominate the Holy Land, but also the place of today's masters—Mohammed's followers—will come (disgrace to the ears of anyone listening!) the most evil among them, the traitor Jews, the killers of our Savior, from whose indecent presence Your Highness and the king your spouse have just freed our country.

Not having completely understood Friar Juan's dream, I asked him to tell me how "the criminal voyage of Columbus" could give back the Holy Land to the Jews. Without being able to explain, he repeated what Saint John the Baptist told him that from Columbus' voyage—if realized—the Jews would receive great profits and finally repossess the Holy Tomb of our Lord.

So, even if the words remain obscure, it is clear that we can believe what this man has to say. He is predicting a terrible calamity if the voyage behind the frontiers designated by the divine providence is realized. I pray and hope that Your Highness will reflect about this somber prophecy revealed and that Your Highness will consent at the very last minute not to support the voyage of this demented Columbus. It is true that I am not an expert on mundane affairs, but I grasp, nevertheless, the one of the reasons explaining the favorable attitude of Your Highness toward Columbus: the fear that this Columbus should address himself to another king, who could make a profit from this criminal plan.

I have already understood your august thoughts, but the Church has in mind to avoid disaster. I have generated contacts with the Saint Inquisition and, to my great joy, I have learned that this noble institution has taken charge of the task "of trying to save the soul of this sinner Columbus."

If Your Highness wishes to confide Columbus into the hands of the Inquisition, I can promise that the floor upon which Columbus will walk will not be the one of a ship. Let the holy Church open Your Highness' eyes so that she can find the right route and be able to save our Church from a great misfortune and the Spanish lands that are under her gracious dominations as well as her soul.

I remain, with emotion, your truthful servant until my death.

Hernando de Talavera

Note: This letter has been contributed by Dr. Michel Pacou on behalf of the Christopher Columbus Philatelic Society in the French language and translated into English by the author.

7

The Ships

It is common knowledge that Columbus left the port of Palos with three caravels; however, according to the documents we have mentioned in chapter five, it appears the possibility that other ships may have been part of the fleet. The term *"caravel"* comprised all similar ships even though some had special peculiarities. The main common features were that they carried a forecastle projecting over the stern and a small poop deck aft. The main mast stood exactly amidst ships. The only other mast was the mizzen, which was stepped in a half deck aft of the main mast. They carried either two lateen (triangular) sails or a square mainsail or a lateen mizzen. The helmsman stood under the half deck and steered with a stern rudder, which was an innovation of this particular period, and a very long tiller.

They were the most common ships sailing the Mediterranean Sea for trade and commercial purposes between the XIV and XVII centuries. Later the Spaniards and the Portuguese used the caravels for exploration. Before being developed for oceanic voyages, there were basically large boats without break-head or stern-castle, having only a simple curved stem and a plain transom stern. The sails were lateen rigged on two masts (*Caravela Latina*). This sail format was an inconvenience for longer oceanic voyages and so caravels were developed into three-mast ships with square rigs on the two fronts masts and a lateen rigged mizzen (*Caravela Rotunda*). This change provided better sail-power balance and avoided lateen sails disabilities caused by the immense length of the yard on which the sail was set and the need of tacking the lower sail in order to bring the yard to the other side of the mast. The overall average length of a three-mast caravel was 75 to 80 feet even though some were built with an overall length of 100 feet.

The *Santa Maria* was at this time better known in Spain as a *nao* (= Spanish word for a regular ship between the XIII and the XVI century) and, because she was Columbus' flagship and he was the Captain on board, she became known as *La Nao Capitana*. She was one of the largest caravels ever built with an overall length of 95 feet. She was a three-mast square-rigged general type of cargo vessel, slow and clumsy and, according to Columbus' statements, not very well suited for voyages of exploration. She carried a crew of 40 men. According to Morison, Columbus renamed her *"Santa Maria"* because her original name was *"Mariagalante"* or *"Marillega."*

The *"Pinta"* (= the painted) was second in size. Always according to Morison, her name came from a member of the Pinto family, who owned her and made it available to Columbus for the voyage. She was a three-mast square-rigged caravel approximately 70 feet in length, with a beam of about 22 feet and a draft of 7. Normally she would carry a crew of about 25 men. She was commanded by Martín Alonso Pinzón.

The *Niña* was the smallest of Columbus' three crafts measuring 67 feet. She was owned by Juan Niño (from whom she took her nickname meaning *"The Little Girl"*) and was built at Moguer. Originally she was named *"Santa Clara"* for the city's patron saint. Juan Niño sailed as Master under the command of Vicente Yáñez Pinzón of Palos. Even though small and with lateen sails, the Niña proved to very quickly to be seaworthy and became the Admiral's favorite ship. She was one of the most advanced ships of her days. In the Canary Islands, however, to take advantage of the oceanic winds and make her even more seaworthy, Columbus changed her sails from lateen to square. When the *Santa Maria* was destroyed on Christmas Day 1492, Columbus used the *Niña* for his voyage of return and many more voyages later on.

In addition to Columbus' three famous ships the documents before the departure as the one after his return indicate quite a few time the presence of another type of caravel called *Fusta*. This type of ship had been used, before the discovery of the New World, in the Mediterranean by the Turks, the Moors, the Duke of Savoy, and the Venetians since the year 1381. The Portuguese began to use her in the Atlantic along the African coast by the *"Ladrones de Mar"* (= Pirate of the sea). The main characteristic of this ship was that she had a deep cargo-hold, could carry quite a bit of weight, a crew up to 40 men, and could withstand strong ocean winds because it had more than three masts and square sails. In regular times the *Fustas* were used for pirates' raids; in war times they were issued letters of qualifications to become part of armadas to officially validates the pirates' activities that could benefit the war. By the time Columbus was ready to undertake his expedition of discovery, apparently the *Fustas* had also become part of the Spanish fleets to be mentioned so many times in the different documents. Nowhere, however, it is mentioned who equipped the Fusta that followed Columbus on his first trip; probably they were independent entrepreneurs or even the same *"Ladrones"* who needed to find other opportunities of trade and commerce once the raids' usual territories had become colonies under government regulations.

Sketch of La Santa Maria.
Museo de Las Casas Reales, Santo Domingo.

Sketch of La Pinta.
Museo de Las Casas Reales, Santo Domingo.

La Niña with lateen sails.

La Niña with square sails.

Sketches at Museo de Las Casas Reales, Santo Domingo.

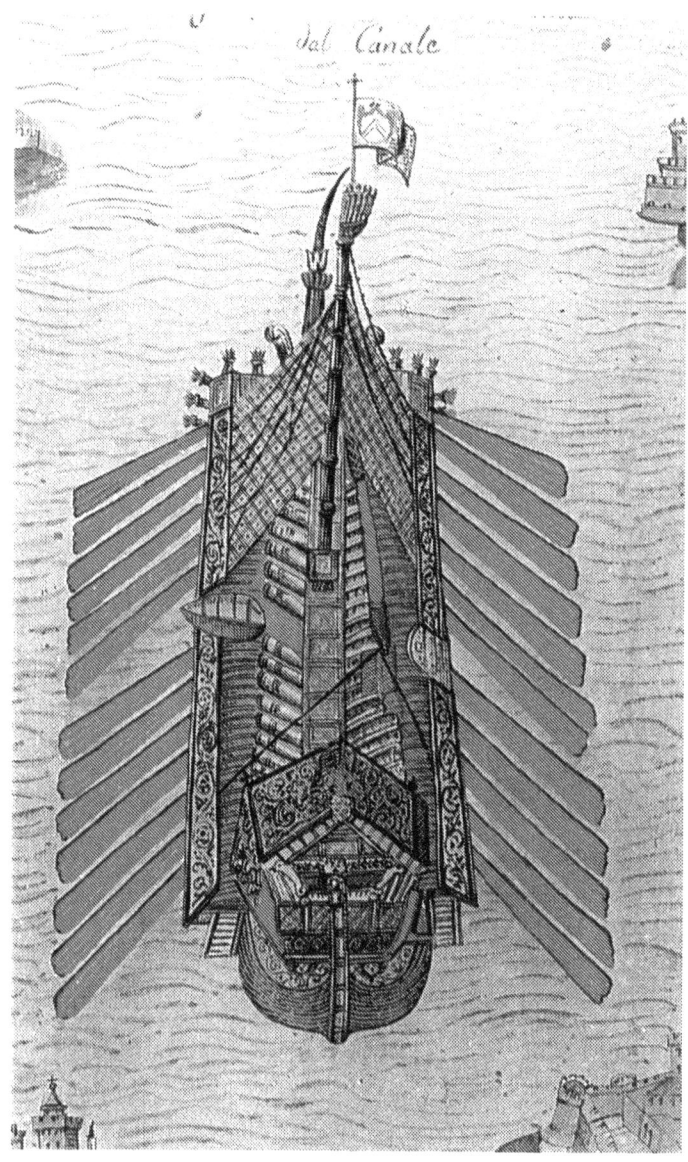

La Fusta used by Spain and Portugal in the
Mediterranean Sea before 1492.
(Courtesy of the Cultural Attaché at the Spanish Consulate in Miami)

La Fusta used by Venetians in the Mediterranean Sea.
(Courtesy of the Cultural Attaché
at the Spanish Consulate in Miami)

La Fusta in a picture at Museo de Las Casas Reales,
Santo Domingo.

BIBLIOGRAPHY

Juan Tomas Tavares K.:" *Ladrones de mar.*" Pp. 105-108. Editora de Santo Domingo S.A. Printed in Spain in 1984.

8

The Crews

The ordinance directed to the Palos' citizens instructed them to equip two caravels. The city's inhabitants had been accused and judged guilty of having offended King Ferdinand and Queen Isabella; therefore, they had been fined and charged with equipping two caravels, to be put at the service of the Crown, with arms and provisions for two years at their own expenses. The said caravels had to be remitted within ten days from the date of the ordinance to Christopher Columbus, who at the same time was equipping the *Santa Maria* on his own.

The Notary Francesco Fernández read the ordinance on the 23rd of May, 1492 in the Church of St. George in Palos in the presence of the authorities and Father Juan Pérez, who had been very important in Columbus' life and very influential in convincing the Spanish Monarchs to undertake this enterprise. This ordinance was quite a shock for the city officials because the Monarchs were not giving a clear explanation of the events to come.

Trusting completely a foreigner to cross an ocean to accomplish such a mission for Spain was too much to ask from expert sailors who were foreseeing their lives and their vessels put in grave danger. But Columbus as well as the Sovereigns had already considered such reaction, since another ordinance, which allowed the suspension of all criminal and civil cases in favor of whoever would embark, accompanied the first.

The Admiral was foreseeing the probable difficulties he would encounter in outfitting the fleet especially because all details had to remain secret. He also knew that in Palos he would encounter even more difficulties because the authorities on experienced navigation were the brothers Pinzón. The Pinzóns were three brothers—Martín Alonso, Francisco Martín, Vicente Yáñez. Martín Alonso was co-owner and Captain of *La Pinta* and his brother Francisco was the Pilot. Vicente was the Captain of *La Niña* during the initial voyage of discovery of the new lands. They were part of a Spanish family of renowned ship-owners and experienced navigators residents of Palos in Andalusia.

Columbus had already met Martín Alonso about his project and had found him favorable to the possibility of collaboration. But after this meeting Columbus changed his mind and decided to organize the expedition on his own, even if it meant to include criminals in the crew and face the brothers Pinzón. Probably this change was due to the fact that the documents about his titles and honors were uncertain, or in other words, not completely legal until the discovery had taken place.

Columbus at this point did not want to lose any earned merit or honor by sharing them with others. He was a foreigner and in the case the brothers Pinzón, being Spanish, had returned from the expedition ahead of him to announce the new discoveries, they would be recognized as the discoverers and Columbus would be forgotten. By mid-June the inhabitants of Palos had not yet executed the order therefore the Crown recalled them. It became clear at this time that until Columbus had reached an agreement with the brothers Pinzón, nobody was going to undertake the outfitting of the caravels. The convicts were only four and the crews were formed of expert sailors.

The *Santa Maria* had 40 men of which 39 are listed in Columbus' log; the *Pinta* had 26 seamen; the Niña 22 seamen. A Captain commanded every ship, however, in the case of the *Santa Maria*, whose Master and owner was Juan de la Cosa, Columbus was the Admiral of the fleet and the Commander on board.

Vicente Pinzón was Captain of the *Niña* until Columbus took over after the *Santa Maria* was shipwrecked. Historians have always disputed the role of the brothers Pinzón in this voyage of discovery. Their participation was decisive in convincing the sailors of Palos, Huelva, and Moguer to overcome the fear of the "*Dark Sea.*"

The most important personality on board was the Pilot, who was responsible for keeping the course. He could read maps, use all instruments of navigation, and many times he was the sole expert in knowing the action of the tides. On the *Santa Maria* Columbus was the only person capable of overseeing the pilot's functions due to the experience acquired in his early years at the service of the King of Portugal.

Others with significant tasks included the Boatswain, who was Lieutenant to the Master or Captain and was in charge of carrying out their orders by distributing the work among the men, setting the sails, and doing general cleaning and maintenance.

The Notary was basically a recorder of the possession-taking of discovered lands and the loading and the unloading to and from the vessels.

The Marshal was in charge of rationing the potable water and could assume authority of judge in disputes, quarrels, and even crimes with power of punishing and condemning.

The Comptroller kept account of the expenses and was responsible for the crown's share of gold.

The Steward rationed the food and the wine. He also oversaw the trimming of the lamps, the building of fires, and the turning over of the sandglasses.

The other tradesmen in the crew were performing individual tasks according to their trades. The masters and the pilots received 20,000 maravedís per month, the expert sailors 1,000, and the ship-boys 666.

The condemned men who enjoyed the royal pardon for participating in this voyage of discovery were only four: Bartolomé Torres, who had been condemned for killing a man in a quarrel. The other three—Alonso Clavijo, Juan de Moguer, and Pedro Yzquierdo de Lepe—were guilty of organizing an escape from jail.

The three crews were formed of mostly Spaniards, except for five exceptions: Columbus and ship-boy Jacomo el Rico from Genoa, Italy; ship-boy Juan Arias from Portugal; seaman Antonio Calabrese from Calabria, Italy; and seaman Giovanni Vecano from Venice, Italy. Among the Spaniards one was from Murcia, 10 from Galicia and the Pays Basque, and the remaining 70 from Andalusia.

Martín and Vicente Pinzón brought with them a younger brother; the Niños were father and son; the Quinteros were two brothers; the Perézes were uncle and nephew; the Arráezes were father and son; the Medeles were two brothers.

Juan de la Cosa, Master and Owner of La Santa Maria.
Portrait at Museo Maritimo, Madrid.

Martín Alonso Pinzón. Captain of la Pinta.
Portrait at Museo Maritimo, Seville.

Vicente Yáñez Pinzón, Captain of La Niña.
Portrait at Museo Maritimo, Madrid.

BIBLIOGRAPHY

Paolo   Emilio   Taviani:*"Cristoforo   Colombo."*   Pp.125-127.   Instituto Geografico de Agostini, Novara, Italy.

9

Life aboard a Caravel

Susceptible to the sea's merciless forces and utterly depending upon the winds, sailors, during the age of the caravels, took comfort in religious ceremonies. The officers who stood watch on the high rear deck placed the images of the saints along the rails to give them solace. This practice led to the term poop deck from the Latin word *"Pupa"* (=Doll).

On a typical day a cabin boy chanting a blessing announced the dawn, then the sailors recited the *Pater Noster* and the *Ave Maria* on deck. When the seventh hourglass was turned over (ca. 6:30 a.m.) the cabin boy wished everyone a good day with another chant. By the next turn of the hourglass it was 7:00 a.m. and the beginning of the workday.

Before the beginning of the first night watch, a boatswain put out the fire and at the turning of the next hourglass, indicating the beginning of the night watch, he wished good night to everyone with another chant.

The sailor's daily routine included mopping the bridge, braiding oakum, mending sails, pumping the bilge, and doing different chores subdivided into watches.

This daily routine was modified on Saturday with the singing of the *Salve Regina* and the reciting of the litanies. After such recitations the master invited everyone to recite the *Apostolic Creed*.

Bureaucracy was also a very important part of life on board. Historians have called Spain *"The Paper Empire"* because of the enormous record keeping and attention for details. Everything was recorded in several copies even when at sea in the cabins of the officials.

The lodging, on a regular size caravel, was the following: the officers slept on pallets over mats below the deck near the rudder. The master, the pilot, and perhaps the marshal and the notary had small separate apartments away from the hold. The seamen slept in a corner of the deck or castle. They were forbidden to sleep in the hold to be able to respond promptly to emergencies.

On the *Santa Maria* the lodgings were completely different. After the ship had been built and equipped for the expedition, at least one third of the deck was modified to lodge the Admiral in dignity. The cabin reserved for Columbus was very simply furnished: it had a table, a chair, a stool, a trunk, a strongbox, writing material and tableware, wash basin, and canopy bed. The walls were decorated with motifs such as shields, armors, swords, navigational instruments, the flags of Castile and Léon, and the image of our Lady of Guadalupe, to whom Columbus was very devoted.

The *Santa Maria* had a large crew and the state of discipline used in the other caravels could not be maintained in the same manner. Personal effects were kept in community chests of different sizes according to the different ranks. The discovery of hammocks used by the Taínos Indians solved the problems for the sailors on large ships.

The food that was provided for a year was water, wine, oil, vinegar, salt, flour, hardtack, lard, pork fat, lentils, onions, fava beans, garlic, olives, dried fish and dried meat, rice, sugar, jams, honey, cheese, almonds, raisins and other dried fruits. During the stop in Gomera, in the Canary Islands, were added livestock (goats). They were fed dried grass and killed sporadically during the voyage to provide fresh meat.

Lunch was served at 11:00 a.m. before the changing of the watch. The officers ate at a table unlike the seamen, who collected their food near the stove holding their bowls and handing them to the servers to be filled; then they ate while sitting on the floor in the most comfortable place they could find.

The sailors did not wear uniforms. The casual outfit was a cape with hood, breeches, a vest with mandarin sleeves with the coat of arms of Spain embroidered on the breast, and also a red cape made of plain cotton cloth instead of wool. These quasi-uniforms were made in Toledo and probably Columbus had more than the crew could use because he gave some to the Indians. Columbus, most of the time, wore a red outfit and a gray cape that was made by Franciscan monks.

Sailor Uniform.
Casa de Colón in Gomera.

BIBLIOGRAPHY

Paolo Emilio Taviani*: **"*Cristoforo Colombo*."** Pp. 125-127. Instituto Geografico de Agostini, Novara, Italy.

10

The Instruments

When Columbus undertook his voyage trying to find a way across the unmarked ocean, it was more a matter of art than science. Sailors in the Middle Ages followed the movements of the stars and the direction of the wind. When the compass was invented it became possible to sail an unknown sea without fear of the fog and the clouds hiding the stars, especially Polaris. Navigating along the coast it was not always necessary to rely on instruments because land was always in sight. But more complex and precise instruments became necessary when ships began to sail the open ocean. Still, even with instruments, sailing directions, and charts ships very frequently ended up off course.

The latitude could be calculated fairly accurately, but the longitude was another story. Without a precise time-keeping device (the chronometer) a ship's position East-West of the principal meridian was just too difficult to determine. When landfall was anticipated, the ship spent the night anchored to avoid running aground. The astrolabe had been so far the main navigation instrument. With it navigators could measure the angle of the sun or of the polar star from the horizon.

The compass indicated the ship's course; her position could be estimated by measuring the speed and the course and, whitin sight of land, certain familiar points could also identify her position. In uncharted and unfamiliar waters the depth of the waters was measured with a *"sounding lead"* (aplomb) known as *"dipsey"* or *"deep sea lead."*

The invention of the mariner's compass was the most important invention to solve all problems. With this instrument became possible to know the direction of the North and relate to it the scuttle of the ship.

From a maritime point of view the discovery of America was the result of advancement of mathematical calculations and perfection of instruments such as the compass with magnetic needle, the forestaff, the astrolabe, and the portable sundial. All these factors made possible Columbus' voyage.

The "*Urca*" (= Hooker, Dogger) used by Spain in the Mediterranean was a derivation of the old Roman *"vasa maritima"* to which succeeded the caravel for Atlantic voyages because it comprised a keel, a lateen sail, and a movable helm. After Columbus, the modification of the *Santa Maria* from caravel to *nao* inspired the creation of new ships like frigates and galleons.

From a social point of view this discovery was a demographic expansion supported by the Renaissance man's spirit of adventure. Religiously speaking the possibility of evangelization was giving the Church even more universal power. Finally for the nation's economy the finding of new routes to the Indies was fulfilling the European need for precious metals and spices. (Information taken from the panels at the Museo Maritimo in Santo Domingo).

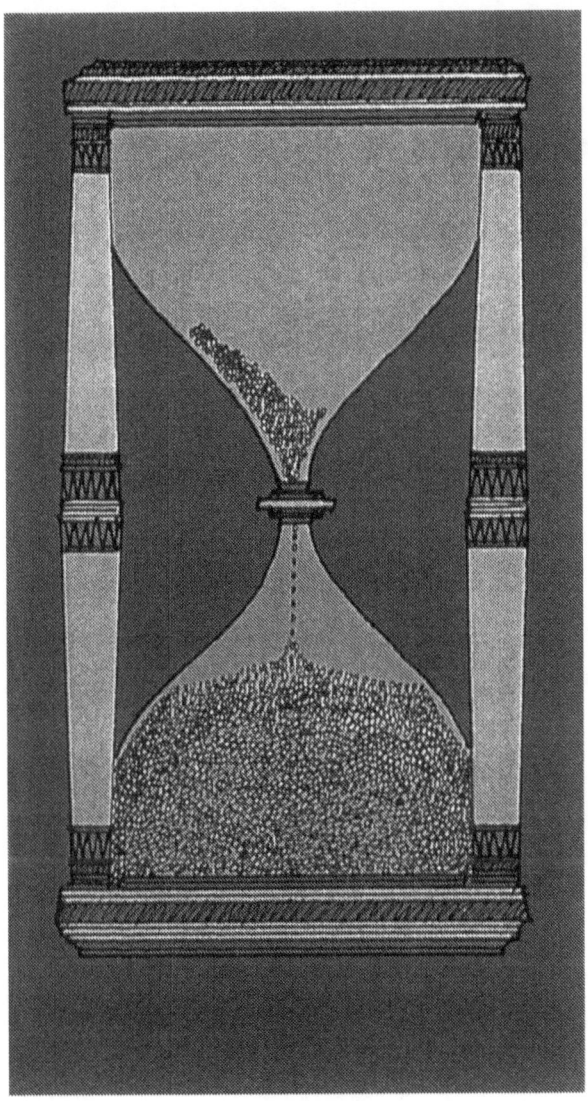

Hour Glass.
Courtesy of the Museo Maritimo in Santo Domingo.

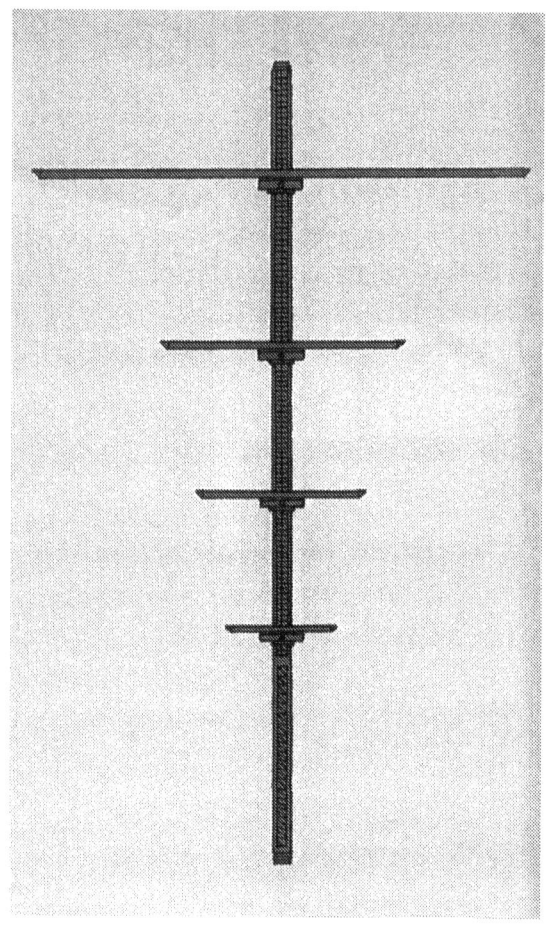

Cross-staff.
Courtesy of the Museo Maritimo in Santo Domingo.

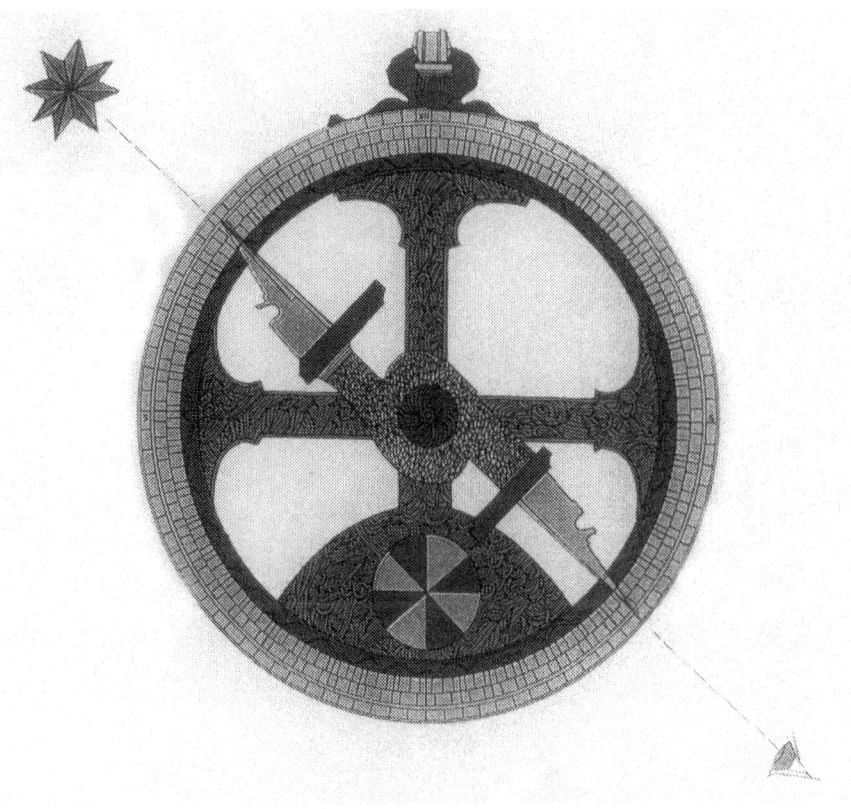

Astrolabe used by Columbus.
Courtesy of the Museo Maritimo in Santo Domingo.

Speed calculator.
Courtesy of the Museo Maritimo in Santo Domingo.

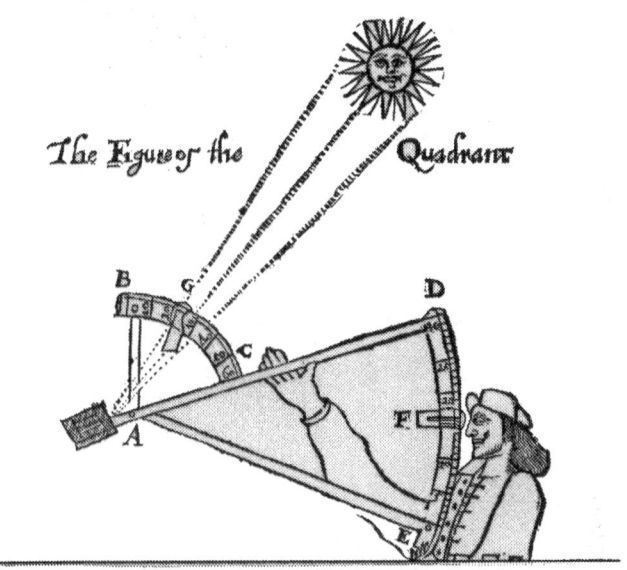

English Quadrant.
(Contributed by Dr. Michel Pacou,
on behalf of the Christopher Columbus Philatelic Society)

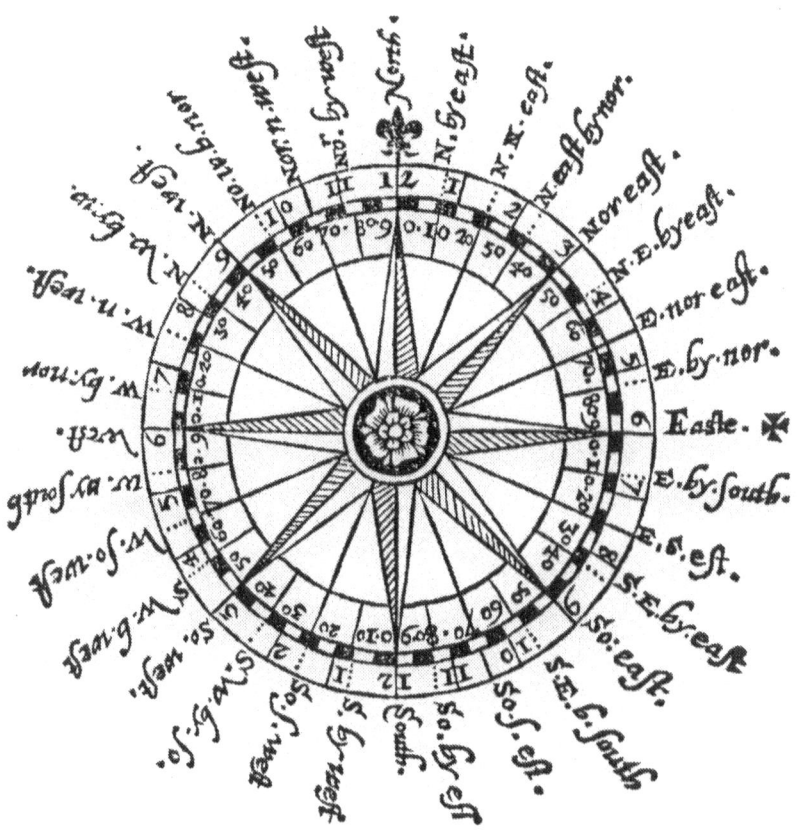

Compass rose.
Courtesy of the Museo Maritimo in Santo Domingo.

11

The Stop at Gomera

When Columbus sailed from Palos on August 3ʳᵈ, 1492, he had already planned to stop at Gomera in the Canary Islands before beginning the crossing of the Atlantic Ocean, because he wanted the help of Beatriz de Bobadilla, Governor of the island. He had met Beatriz at the Spanish court when she was a young girl and Ferdinand's favorite. Her cousin, the Marchioness of Moya and her husband, Andrés de Cabrera, had been a great influence in convincing the queen to understand Columbus' genius and to support his project. Columbus considered them among the group of his court protectors.

Isabella, when she married Ferdinand and became queen, ordered Beatriz to marry Hernán de Peraza, Governor of Gomera, and leave immediately after the wedding. In November of 1488 Hernán was killed by a gang of *Guanches* (= Gomera natives), who could no longer endure his tyranny.

According to Spanish legend the name Gomera was taken from Gomer, Noah's grandson, whose descendents—the Gomerans—populated the island after the Great Flood.

Because of the fertility of this land, Columbus had chosen to stop here to supply the ships with grains, vegetables, and fruits that were growing all year through. But there was also another reason. The Admiral wanted to start the crossing on the same parallel as the Island of Hierro, the same island mentioned in the map drawn by the captain, who had died in his house.

In 1492 all conflicts with Portugal over the ownership of the Canary Islands had ended. The Treaty of Alcaçobas in 1479 and the Peace of Toledo in 1480 had been confirmed by Pope Sixtus IV in his Bull *"Aeterni Regis"* in 1481 by giving to Spain complete ownership of the Canary Islands. However in 1492 the Guanches still occupied Tenerife and La Palma Islands. In other words, Spain's Sovereignty had been assured only on the other islands of the archipelagos. After her husband's death, Beatriz de Peraza became Governor of Gomera and more interested in affairs of state than in her family. She had been in September of

1491 in Cordoba and in November of the same year in Seville; then in May of 1492 in Santa Fé and had received from the Monarchs the order of helping Columbus.

"*On the 9th of August La Pinta reached the Grand Canary in the morning and I ordered Martín Alonso to remain here until the caravel could be properly repaired and the rudder replaced. I took La Santa Maria and La Niña and set to Gomera.*" (Excerpt from "The Log").

Punta Salina in the Grand Canary.

Columbus arrived in Gomera on the 12th of August 1492 and stayed here until the 23rd when "*…. He resolved on the 23rd of August to return with his two ships to the Grand Canary: and leaving on the following day he could not arrive to the Grand Canary due to severe head winds. He picked up the ship's guide and spent the night near Tenerife, from whose mountains large flames were seen that amazed the men; they were given to understand the cause of the fire, comparing it Mount Etna of Sicily and of other such mountains where the same was seen.*" (Excerpt from "*Historia del Almirante*" by Diego Colón).

El Teide, the highest mountain in Tenerife, was a volcano and was in the process of erupting. Columbus returned to Gomera and stayed here another eleven days—from the 23rd of August to the 6th of September. La Pinta, which had been already repaired by the 23rd of August, came to Gomera and remained docked with the other caravels in San Sebastián until the day of the beginning of the crossing.

During Columbus' stay in Gomera, some historians said that he was "*touched by love*" for Doña Beatriz. It is certain, however, that she helped him with the provisions and provided food and accommodations for him in her house.

Here in Gomera Columbus needed help in converting the *Niña's* sails from lateen to square to make her even swifter and responsive to the ocean winds. So Beatriz found many noble Spaniards—fact that surprised Columbus—willing to help. Even though the Canary Islands were also known as "*The Fortuna Isles*" they were a poor country and the only known society was the native Guanches. However this matter was later clarified by the fact that, after studies on the Guanches Society, it was discovered that from the time the Canaries Islands had become Spanish possessions, the Guanches had submitted to the crown of Castile and adopted Catholicism and the Castilian language. So even though without riches generated by gold, silver, and other precious metals some of the Guanches became nobility because of the amount of land and livestock owned.

By Joseph Viera y Clavijo. Title page.

Doña Beatriz de Bobadilla Peraza.
(Portrait at El Parador, San Sebastián, Gomera)
Photo contributed by Dr. Michel Pacou on behalf of the
Christopher Columbus Philatelic Society.

BIBLIOGRAPHY

Paolo Emilio Taviani: *"The Grand Design"* p. 483. Instituto Geografico de Agostini, Novara, Italy.

Paolo Emilio Taviani: *"The Great Discovery"* pp. 38-40. Instituto Geografico de Agostini, Novara, Italy.

Discovery: *"Journal of the Christopher Columbus Philatelic Society"* Vol. 25, p. 1715 and 1721.

12

The Letter to Santángel

On March 4, 1493 Columbus had returned from his voyage of discovery: exactly seven months and one day since his departure from Palos. The Admiral had come back on board of the *Niña* and landed in Lisbon. He was very anxious to let the Spanish Monarchs know about his discoveries because he had lost sight of the *Pinta* commanded by Martín Alonso Pinzón already docked at Baiona, a small port on the Northeast coast of Spain, and feared that he would claim the right of discovery. Columbus arrived at Palos on March 15 and the *Pinta* arrived on the same day a few hours after Columbus.

By the time Columbus had made a short stop at the Azores Islands, he had prepared *"Las Relaciones,"* a report to be sent to all the influential personalities at court. But the report to Luis de Santángel, in letter format, remains the most important and famous for including all the topics of *"Las Relaciones"* plus more details. Columbus wrote:

"My Lord,

Because I know that you will have pleasure in knowing about the great victory that God has granted me during this voyage, I write to you this letter in which you will learn how in thirty-four days I have gone from the Canary Islands to the Indies with the fleet that the illustrious king and queen have given me. Here I have found a great number of islands, populated by many inhabitants, of which I have taken possession in the name of Their Highnesses with legal proclamation and royal flags without encountering opposition. To the first island by me discovered I have given the name of San Salvador in honor of the omnipotent God who has created so many marvels. The Indians call this island "Guanahani." I gave the second island the name of "Santa Maria de la Concepción" and to the third the name "Fernandina." I called the fourth "Isabela" and the fifth "Juana" and many different other names to all the ones I have discovered. (Santa Maria de la Concepción is called today Rum Cay, Fernandina is Long Island, Isabela is formed by two islands called Crooked and Fortune separated by a strait in which is found a third islet called Bird Rock. Juana is today's Cuba).

When I arrived to Juana, I sailed along the west side of the coast and I found it so large that I thought it was part of Cathay. But because I could not find any villages, except for a couple of fishermen's huts inhabited by few men, who began to flee as soon as they spotted us, we continued to sail hoping to find a village or a city soon. After having gone quite a few leagues and noticed that the coast was offering no possibilities, against my will and because winter was approaching and winds were also against us, I kept sailing north to go back to a port I had already spotted and sent two men on land to discover whether there were large cities nearby.

After a three-day march they found many villages with plenty of inhabitants who had no government and so they came back to the ship. Finally from some Indians I had captured, I was able to understand that the land was an island and I decided to sail around its coast toward east for a length of 107 leagues up to the place where it was forming a promontory. (At this point Columbus thought to have reached Cathay according to the description of the land given by Marco Polo, but, not having found the city of Cipango, he realized he had failed).

On the east of this cape, 18 leagues from the first island, I found another island that I called Española, I directed the ship toward it and sailed along the coast on the north side for a length of one hundred eighty-eight leagues as I did along the coast of Juana. This isle, as well as the others, is very fertile. It has infinity of natural ports, which cannot be compared to any other in the Christian lands for beauty and location and many rivers just marvelous to look at. The configuration of Española is exceptional; there are very high mountain chains much higher than Tenerife. They are simply majestic and various. All of them are accessible and covered with trees so tall that seem to touch the sky. It seems to me that these trees do not lose their leaves because I have always seen them green and as beautiful as the trees in Spain during the month of May. Some were even in bloom and some had fruits. I could hear the birds singing in a thousand different ways wherever I was going even though it was November. There are six or eight different species of palm trees and I am ecstatic to look at all these varieties of plants. There are marvelous pine forests and fields; there is honey, many species of birds and fruits never seen before. Inland there are mines and quite a few inhabitants. Española is simply stupendous: the mountains, the valleys, the plains are so fertile that anything can be planted, cattle can be raised and cities and villages can be built. The ports on the ocean are of extreme beauty; the rivers are many and quite large with pure waters that in many cases carry gold. Here the vegetation is different than in Juana where there are many types of spices and mines of gold and different other metals.

The inhabitants of this island, as the ones of all the others, are naked even though some of the women cover the superior parts of their bodies with tree leaves or with a piece of cloth woven especially for this purpose. They do not use iron or steel to make arms because they are shy. The only arms they know are made out of bamboo picked after the blooming season on which extremities they attach a piece of wood very pointy. Many times they do not even use this weapon. In fact I was able to drag to the ground two or three men who were approaching to speak with us and the ones, who were coming to protect them, fled as soon as they saw this happen. No harm had been done to any of them because everywhere I have gone I have brought presents with me without receiving anything in return. They are so shy that it is not possible to approach them, but once they have been reassured that no harm is done to them they are so generous and hospitable that nobody can believe it unless they see it with their own eyes. They never refuse what is demanded from them and, when in possession of an object we like and want, they cannot wait to give it to us with great friendship. They are always very happy no matter how cheap is the object we give them in exchange. I had to forbid my men to give them objects of no value like broken dishes, pieces of glass, strips of ribbon even though they think that these items are precious. It happened that one of the sailors received a gold nugget valued at two and a half "Castellanos" (= ancient Spanish coin) *for just a piece of colorful ribbon and many other sailors received much more than what they had exchanged was worth. Many times for a new "Blanca"* (= old Spanish copper coin) *these Indians gave all they owned up to the value of two or more "Castellanos" or one or more "Arroba"* (= unit of weight equivalent to 25 lbs. or 11.5 kilos) *of cotton thread. The sailors were exchanging anything they could find including pieces of broken kegs and pieces of scrap metal like real animal to the point that I had to stop this dishonest trading. I gave to these natives many of my valuable objects that I had brought with me for the purpose of making them friends and convert them to Christianity; to make them love Their Highnesses and the whole Castilian nation so they could procure and remit to us the products that they have in abundance and we need so much.*

These Indians do not profess any particular kind of religion nor they know idolatry. They believe that every power and every goodness comes from the sky; they also believe that even I with my ships and my men have come from the sky and because of such belief they have received us in a friendly manner after their first fears had gone. Such sentiments do not stem from ignorance. These Indians are very intelligent. They can navigate the seas and explain everything in a terrific manner, but they have never seen our kinds of ships nor men dressed in clothes. As soon as we landed on the first island, I took some by force to have them tell me everything that could be found on it and so it happened that quite fast we were able to understand each other in words and gestures.

This way these men have rendered great service. I am holding them with me even now and they still believe that I have come from the sky. Wherever we land they want to be the first to announce the news going from house to house screaming: "Come to see the men from the sky!" Men, women, and children, after having been reassured that it was safe to meet us, came to bring us food and drinks with incredible amiability.

They have in all islands canoes with oars made like our fustas, some smaller, some longer, and some even longer than a fusta with eighteen benches, but not very large because they are carved out of a single tree trunk, and extremely fast to outdo our fustas. With these crafts they go from island to island to transport their merchandise. I have seen enter in one from sixty to eighty men, each one at an oar. In these islands I have not noticed a difference in their customs nor in their language—they all understand each other. I hope that Their Highnesses will take care of their conversion to the Christian faith to which they seem to be very inclined.

I have already explained how I have navigated 107 leagues along the coast of Juana from west to east and, basing my knowledge on this experience, I can say that Juana is larger than England and Scotland together because, beside the 107 leagues, on the west side there are still two provinces to be yet explored, one of which is called "Avan" where the inhabitants have tails. These two provinces must be at least another 50 or 60 leagues away from here, according to what I have learned from the Indians still with me who know all these isles. Española measures in perimeter more than Spain following the coast from Colliure to Fuentarrabia in the Gulf of Gascoigne, because in sailing only around one side from west to east, I have covered a distance of 188 great leagues. This place is a dreamland and, after having seen it once, it is difficult to forget it. Even though I have taken possession of all the other islands—that are richer than expected—in the names of Their Highnesses so they can dispose as they please for the benefit of Spain, this island Española, I say, is the best place to exploit for its gold mines. To start commerce between the two continents, I have taken possession of a great village called "Village Navidad" where I have begun to build a fenced-in fort that should be finished by now. Here I have left a sufficient number of men with arms, artillery, provisions for a year, and the fusta with the Master Mariner and other tradesmen to become friends with the king of the island. This king felt very honored to consider us brothers and, even if he would change his mind, his subjects, not used to arms or armors because they are always naked, can easily be destroyed with the amount of ammunitions I have left for this purpose. It is an island where our men will not incur in any kind of danger as long as they know how to behave themselves. In all these islands it seems that the men are happy with only one wife, while the Chief or King can have up to twenty. The women work harder than the men. I have not been able to find out whether they own personal property. It seems that everything is commonly owned, especially the food.

In these islands I have not found monstrous men as commonly believed. They all have an agreeable appearance and they are not black as the inhabitants of Guinea, except that they have long and affluent hair, which does not grow where the body is most exposed to the powerful sunrays. The sun here is very strong because we are only 26 degrees away from the Equator, but where there are mountains, the winter cold is very pungent. The natives are tolerating this cold by ingesting spicy food.

We have not yet seen any monsters. There is only one island, the second at the entrance to the Indies, where the population is believed to be very fierce and eating human flesh. These natives possess many canoes to go on raids to the other islands, rob, and kill as much as they can. They are not less handsome than the others, but they wear their hair long and tied in a ponytail like the women. They use bows and arrows made from pointed pieces of wood for lack of iron. They are ferocious compared to the other populations, but I do not consider them more dangerous than any others. These are the ones who have rapports with the women of "Matinino", the first island encountered coming from Spain, because there are no men where these women live. These women do not occupy themselves with feminine duties, but they know how to use bows and arrows and they protect their bodies with a sheet of copper, a very abundant metal in the island.

I have also learned that there is another island even bigger than Española where the people have no hair in any part of their bodies. In this island there is much gold and I am bringing with me some men from it as witnesses. In conclusion, Their Highnesses will see that what has been accomplished from this voyage is the fact that I can give them all the gold they need if they will help me. Even more spices, cotton, gum mastic of the quality that up to today has been only found in the isle of Chio in Greece to be sold at a very high price, aloe woods, and slaves chosen among the idolaters. I also think to have found rhubarb and cinnamon and I will find even more precious merchandise thanks to the persons I have left there. When the winds were propitious I kept on sailing and did not stop in any particular port to investigate, except for Village Navidad where I landed and paused to leave everything in order. I could have accomplished even more if the vessels had been more apt to my needs. Most of this enterprise should not be attributed to the genius and industry of the human race, but to the intercession of God, who grants victory to everyone, who relies on his help in impossible enterprises. And ours was certainly one of those!

Everything was based on conjectures not on proven experience, and everyone who was listening knew that this whole project could have been only an illusion. So it was the powerful hand of the Redeemer that gave this victory to our illustrious king and queen and their realms, which will become famous. The Christian Community should rejoice with great feasts and thank the Holy Trinity with prayers for the increment that it will receive from the conversion of all these peoples to our faith as well as from the earthly goods from which not only Spain, but also the whole world can benefit. I am reporting in a very brief manner everything that has been accomplished.

Written on board of the Niña near the Canary Islands the 15ᵗʰ of February 1493.

The Admiral."

"*After having written this letter and still on board of my ship in the Sea of Castile I was attacked by such strong winds that I had to lighten it. Today I have stopped in the port of Lisbon, from where I have decided to write to Their Highnesses, to make repairs generating great astonishment. In all the Indies I have witnessed storms like the ones in Spain during the Month of May. I went there in 33 days and I returned in 28. In this sea here, however, these tempests have retarded my arrival of 14 days. All seamen say that the winter has been very severe and there have been so many shipwrecks.*

Written on the 4ᵗʰ of March 1493."

This letter is very important because it has reached us as it was originally written, without the kind of manipulation in transcription or translation, as sometimes it happens in copies. It can also be considered an official document because it is written as a report (= relación) to a very important personality at court with the intention to make it public. It acquired also the value of a legal document.

Courtesy of Christopher Columbus Philatelic Society

Courtesy of the Christopher Columbus Philatelic Society

BIBLIOGRAPHY

Marinella Bonvini Mazzanti: *"1492: Scoperta e conquista dell'America."* Pp. 121-122. Studi Storici Universitá di Urbino, Italy.

Marinella Bonvini Mazzanti: *"1492: Scoperta e conquista dell'America."* Pp. 124-126. Studi Storici Universitá di Urbino, Italy.

13

The Taíno Society

From Columbus' letter to Santángel we know that the isles discovered in 1492 are known today as the Archipelago of the Antilles, which extends from the peninsula of Yucatán (Mexico) to the North Coast of Venezuela. With the exception of the Bahamas, located on the North Coast of Santo Domingo and Cuba, the mentioned isles are in the Tropic of the Cancer, which includes the Gulf of Mexico and the Caribbean Sea.

The total area of these islands is more that 237.000 square kilometers. They are divided in two groups: the Major and the Minor Antilles. The first group includes Cuba (originally named by Columbus Juana), the Dominican Republic (originally named Española) comprising Santo Domingo and Haiti, Jamaica and finally Puerto Rico. Cuba, which is the largest of this group, measures ca. 114,425 square kilometers.

The Minor Antilles comprise a more numerous group of islands subdivided in Sotovento and Barlovento in accordance with their nautical position. The principal are: Sombrero, Perro, San Martin, San Bartholomew, Barbuda, Saba, San Eustaquio, San Cristobál, Nevis, Antigua, Monserrat, Guadalupe, Deseada, Tierra Pequeña, Santos, Mariagalante, Dominica, Martinica, Santa Lucia, San Vicente, Granada, Granadinas, Barbados, Tobago, Trinidad, Testigos, Curazao, Bonaire, Aruba.

In the Bahamas the most important is the Grand Bahamas. The others are: Gran Abaco, Moose, Berry, Bimini, Adros, Espiritu Santo, Nueva Providencia, Eleuthera, Gato, San Salvador, Rum, Long, Gan, Exuma, Grand Guanacay, Aclin, Planas, Samana, Mariguana, Caicos, Turcas, Grand Inagua, Pequeña Inagua. The Antilles present a great contrast because of the difference in language, in population, political and social conditions—all this representing a varied history. The isle of Santo Domingo measures 77,000 square kilometers and is subdivided in two parts: Dominican Republic and Haiti.

Before the arrival of the Spaniards three groups of natives lived in these islands. The *Ciboneys* lived in caves and in dwellings made out of stones laid one on top of another. Their names derive from the word *ciba* (= stone) and *eyen* (= man). The second group was the *Taínos,* who lived in Puerto Rico, Santo Domingo and Haiti. These Indians formed the major part of the population—ca. 200 to 300 millions—and were the ones who came in contact with Columbus. Their riches were not provided by mines of gold and silver, as erroneously believed, but by nutritional food, medicinal herbs, natural beverages, plants from which to extract dyes, and habits that were *"a pure treasure of hospitality, trust, and friendship."* (From Columbus' log page 153).

Among the novelties found by Columbus in the Antilles that began to invade Europe during the XVI century were tobacco, a beverage made with cocoa beans roasted, ground, and mixed with water, pepper and spices, which became known as chocolate. To all this we must add the hammock. The Admiral, Bartolomé de Las Casas, Oviedo, and Peter Martyr described the hammock and the way to make it in the same manner the Taínos were making it. They lived permanently in large villages organized in *"Cacigazcos"* under the authorities of at least three categories of *"Caciques"* and specialists in religious and medical rites.

They lived in dwellings called *"Buhios"* that were of two different types. The most common were called *"Caney"* with a conic roof supported by pillars surrounding a central one that divided it in two parts. This type of construction was covered with large leaves of yaguas and bejucos bushes. The other type of dwelling was rectangular and roomier constructed with the same material but used exclusively by the chiefs of the villages. The roof had two levels and the most important dwellings had an antechamber where the guests were received. In these large dwellings the women were making terracotta vases, raffia baskets, and kitchen utensils. Their rich and mythological heritage, accompanied by a very sharp artistic sense, was expressed in their woven fabrics, woodcarvings, and ceramic work.

Columbus reported in the Log his surprise when he met Cacique Guacanagari, who sent his subjects to help the sailors unload the provisions from the Santa Maria, after she was shipwrecked, and put them in a safe place. Columbus reciprocated this favor with plenty of presents worthy of his position and received him on board. Another fact that surprised the Admiral was that not only the *Cacique* but also his people trusted fully Columbus and were so hospitable to demonstrate a high level of social culture. This high level of social culture, trust and frankness became a consequence of the discovery that brought a temporary fusion of the races.

In Taíno society an "*India Nataína*" was a woman of high social class. She could also marry a Spanish of low social class and give him nobility title making him owner of many "*noborias*" (= handy workers) and incorporate him in her family. Many women were taken by force, but many others were completely consenting to marry a Spaniard and have a legitimate union through a special rite. That made the man part of her family and the Taíno society.

These unions began a process called "*Mestizaje*" (= half-breed) because the new generation of children born from two different races—Taíno woman and white Spaniard—created a third human race which was a mixture. Oviedo writes: "*The Taíno family was monogamous. Only the Caciques or the Great Chiefs were polygamous.*" The man was the head of the family, but matriarchal laws regulated the succession. When the man died, the eldest son assumed the physical responsibility of guiding the family. If a couple did not have successors, the eldest son of the dead man's sister was becoming the head of the family.

A typical characteristic of the Taíno society—certainly worthy of mention—was the special solidarity between the members of the different clans within the village. Very rarely quarrels started between neighbors and, when a man wanted to marry a woman, he had to buy her from her family with costly presents. But the Taínos had to realize very soon that the hospitality they offered to the Spaniards was not reciprocated. The 39 men left at Fort Navidad began to pillage the gold and silver mines and rape the girls.

This created a rebellion commanded by Cacique Caonabó who wanted to chase the foreigners from his land. Cacique Guacanagari tried to help the strangers because of the friendship with Columbus, but he was not sufficiently powerful to overcome Caonabó's forces and followers. So Columbus sent a platoon of soldiers commanded by Don Pedro Margarite to Cibao, which was the *Cacigazo* of Cacique Guarionex in a region called by the natives Magua to which Columbus gave the name of *Vega Reál* (= Regal Plain).

The mission of these soldiers was to build another fort "*Santo Tomás*" and control the rebels. But the situation did not improve; also Marguerite's soldiers began to rape the Taíno women and the rebels ended up decimating them.

Contributed by Dr. Sophie Jakowska.

Columbus showing a Spanish coin to a Taíno Indian.
Painting by Juan Medina Ramirez, Santo Domingo.

Taíno pottery. (Courtesy of Museo de la Universidad Autonoma Santo Domingo).

Taíno pottery.
(Courtesy of Museo de la Universidad Autonoma,
Santo Domingo).

Taíno conic dwelling.
(Contributed by Dr. Sophie Jakowska)

Opyelguobirán: Taíno divinity.
(Contributed by Dr. Sophie Jakowska)

Columbus invoking blessings on Española.
(Courtesy of Columbus Museum in Chicago).

BIBLIOGRAPHY

JOSÉ RAMON ESTELLA (writer): *"Historia Grafica de la Republica Dominicana."* Pp. 2-10. Editora Teller, Santo Domingo.

JOSÉ ALLOZA VILLAGRASA (illustrator): *"Historia Grafica de la Republica Dominicana."* Pp. 3-7. Editora Teller, Santo Domingo.

14

The Return

At his arrival at Lisbon, Columbus went to visit King Juan II of Portugal with the six Indians he had brought with him from the West Indies. When the king realized that they were not the same types as the ones in Guinea from La Mina, he was pleased, but at the same time he regretted not having sponsored the expedition and tried to impede Columbus from reaching Spain. Columbus did not feel any longer safe waiting in Portugal and on March 13, 1493 he sailed for Palos.

In Palos he stayed with Martin Alonso Pinzón at La Rábida monastery until he received news from King Ferdinand on April 7 that he would be received in Barcelona. From Palos he traveled over land to Seville and then to Barcelona.

Bartolomé de Las Casas in his *"Historia de las Indias"* describes Columbus' reception by the Sovereigns as an apotheosis, a terrific grand celebration.

"The people swarmed in the streets all marveling at the sight of this venerable personality who, it is said, had discovered another world and at the sight of the Indians, parrots, objects, gems, and the golden jewelry he bore, which they had never seen before. Many great noblemen from Castile, Cataluña, Valencia, and Aragon, all most anxious to see the arrival of the one who had completed an undertaking so grand that caused rejoicing throughout the Christian world, were waiting with the Sovereigns. Columbus entered the room where the Monarchs were, accompanied by a multitude of knights and nobles. He stood among them like a Roman Senator because of his authoritative stature, his venerable head of gray heir and a modest smile, which increased the pleasure and glory with which he greeted. After kissing the Monarchs' hands and giving a detailed account of the voyage, Columbus presented the Sovereigns with the new subjects and offered them the riches of the newly discovered lands. The ceremony ended with a solemn "Te Deum" intoned by the cantors of the Royal Chapel while the Monarchs knelt and the whole court wept for joy with their hearts filled with thankfulness for the beautiful and numerous gifts."

All the documents drawn in April 1492 assumed now a different value and with this happy return everything changed and doubts vanished. All conditions

89

had been fulfilled. As a reward the Monarchs allowed Columbus to add to his coat of arms the gold Castle of Castile and the purple lion of Léon. On May 28, 1493 in Barcelona the Admiral was named Captain General of the second fleet to depart for the Indies.

While in Barcelona, Columbus wrote letters to his supporters and at the same time he sent a copy of the *La Relación* to Pope Alexander VI as basis for the preparation of the Bull *"Inter caetera."* regarding the Spanish jurisdiction in the new lands. Also he sent to his friend Gabriel Sánchez the same letter he had sent to Luis de Santángel describing the customs of the Indians, their amiability, the natural beauty of the islands, the possibility of finding plenty of gold, spices, precious woods, and finally the construction of Fort Navidad where he left the *fusta* with 39 men. This letter was translated into Latin by Leandro Cosco, a Spanish employee at the Vatican in April 1493 and sent to all European nations.

Cosco translated the word *fustas* as *"item quondam caravellam."* Being a Catalan, Cosco knew the difference between the types of sea vessels used by Spain and also knew that the *fusta* was a pirate ship used in raids. So he used the word caravel thinking that this word would be more appropriate to emphasize the expedition's spirit of evangelization.

There was also the hypothesis that the *fusta* could have been changed into a caravel at Gomera before the crossing of the ocean. The second hypothesis is confirmed in the letter of Annibale de Gennaro, special papal envoy to Barcelona, to his brother Antonio reporting that at court the news was that Columbus had accomplished this enterprise with "four ships."

Also by the time the letter to Sánchez had been translated into Latin and sent all over Europe, everyone in Spain knew from Santángel that Columbus had left the *fusta* at the Fort Navidad in Española. On January 2, 1493 Columbus wrote in his Log: *"I left in this island, that the Indians call Bohío, 39 men in the fortress under the command of three officers all of whom have become very friendly with King Guacanagari. In command is Don Diego de Arana, a native of Cordova, to whom I have given in full all the powers I have received from the Sovereigns. Next in line, if something should happen to him, is his Lieutenant Pedro Gutiérrez, the representative of the Royal Household. Next in line of succession is the Lieutenant Rodrigo de Escobedo, Secretary of the fleet and native of Segovia, nephew of friar Rodrigo Pérez. I also left persons qualified in construction among which Alonso Morales, carpenter; Lope, joiner; Diego Pérez, painter; Chachú, boatswain; Juan de medina, tailor; Domingo Vizcaino, cooper; Maestre Alonso and Maestre Juan, surgeons."*

The fact that two surgeons were left at Fort Navidad further proves that Columbus had four ships. It was a basic rule of navigation that every ship had to have on board a doctor and Columbus would not have attempted such a voyage without the proper number of physicians. He returned with Maestre Diego in the *Pinta* and Maestre Alonso from Moguer in the Niña.

Courtesy of the Christopher Columbus Philatelic Society.

Courtesy of Christopher Columbus Philatelic Society.

The Voyages of Columbus

Reporting Discoveries

Courtesy of the Christopher Columbus Philatelic Society.

15

Annibale de Gennaro's Letter

In 1493 when the exultant news of Columbus' discovery became known, the interests of the European nations switched to the forming of political alliances. From this "*modus operandi*" arose the necessity for the various princes to be informed by diplomatic sources accredited to the different courts. The ambassadors had the duty to send the minutest details about the changes happening at the Spanish court so their Lords would know what to do.

Annibale De Gennaro was in Spain in April 1493, as a special envoy from the Vatican, and had been asked by his brother Antonio, who was the spokesperson for the King of Naples in Milan, to keep him informed about the current Spanish events.

The De Gennaro family had been in the diplomatic service of the King of Naples, Don Ferrante of Aragon King Ferdinand's brother, for many years. Annibale was a cultured person who had traveled extensively; his signature on legal documents was always in Latin, "*Hannibal Januarius*" to make everyone understand how he was sensitive to the humanistic culture and was trying to translate the humanities into the practices of a natural normal daily life. Being at the Court of Spain as the papal special envoy he was able to have access to certain information, which even though secret, at least was reserved for the eyes and ears of a selected few.

His letter reads:

"Honored brother,

*This day I am writing to you before any other messenger receives the order to do so. The month of August of the past year has seen this king, at the request of a certain Columbus, issue an edict to arm and equip **four caravels** for him to navigate the ocean in a direct route to the West through the Strait* (= the Strait of Gibraltar known at the time as "The Columns of Hercules") *and, from the letters I have* *seen, he arrived in 34 days to a great island in which lived human beings with red skin, naked, shy, and without bellicose intent. Some of the men went ashore to find information and learn their language so they could communicate with them. As soon as they were no longer afraid, being quite intelligent, they were making themselves understood through signs and other ways so our men found that they were in the islands of the Indies. These Indians went to their nearest villages to announce that a man sent from God had landed and had met with them in good faith to offer friendship and love. When our men continued their route, after having left this island, they found a quantity of isles among which one larger than England and Scotland together and another larger than Spain. He has left there some men with provisions and ammunitions for a year after having started the construction of a fortress. He came back with six natives so they could learn our language. In these islands he has found pepper, wood, aloe, gold, and many rivers—in other words many rivers carry in their sand gold particles. The natives navigate in canoes whose largest can hold from seventy to eight rowers.*

Columbus has returned and landed in Lisbon. As soon as he landed he wrote to the Monarchs, who urged him to come to Spain as soon as possible. I hope I can be able to see the letter he has written to the Sovereigns so I can send you a copy. And, as soon as he has arrived here, anything else that his letter to the Monarch does not say and that I can hear at court. In this court it is now known that the Indians do not have any type of government, nor that they belong to a sect; they believe that everything comes from the creator and should be easy to convert them to the Christian faith. Columbus also says that he was in a province where men have tails. Don Diego Lopez de Aro will leave tomorrow. He is going to speak in Rome to offer the services of the Spanish Monarchs to Pope Alexander VI, as I have already written to you. He brings with him 60 mules, 20 carriages and plenty of silver; from Rome he will go to Naples. There is nothing else worthy of mention.

Barcelona, 19th of March 1493
Your obedient brother Hannibal Januarius.

We need to observe that De Gennaro wrote "***four caravels***" very clearly in words and not in numbers, indicating so that "*La nao capitana*" as well as "*La Fusta*" had become two new types of vessels in this expedition. A letter of Don Luis de la Cerda Duke of Medinaceli, who had offered hospitality to Columbus many times during his stay in Spain, mentions that, from the very first day, he had been convinced about the validity of Columbus' plan and had offered to put at the stranger's disposal "***four caravels***" of his own fleet. However when he went to court to make this proposal to King Ferdinand and Queen Isabella he received a refusal because the Sovereigns had in their minds that the realization of the enterprise should be automatically the duty of the Crown.

On March 19˙ 1493 the Duke of Medinaceli went to see Cardinal Pedro Gonzáles de Mendoza—who could corroborate his testimony—to remind him of the offer he had made to the Monarchs and how he had interceded for Columbus. This time, however, he wanted to ask the queen for her consent to send to the new lands *"algunas caravelas"* (=some caravels) of his fleet on a yearly basis.

The Duke of Medinaceli was the richest feudal Lord in Spain and by asking to be the first to travel to the new world was giving the Spanish Crown a great success. Columbus' first voyage had been accomplished mostly under the auspices of the Court of Castile, whose authority was only Queen Isabella, before the political union of the two kingdoms had happened.

BIBLIOGRAPHY

Marinella Bonvini Mazzanti: *1492: Scoperta e Conquista dell'America.* " Pp. 150-152. Studi storici Universitá di Urbino, Italy.

G. Berchet: *"Fonti Italiane per la storia del Nuovo Mondo."* P. III, vol. I, p. 141.

Samuel Eliot Morison: *"Cristoforo Colombo."* P. 384.

16

Pope Alexander VI's Bulls

The Spanish ambassador had left in haste to bring the pope the news of Columbus' success. It was believed all over Europe that the division of the new lands would be favorable for Spain because pope Alexander VI was Spanish. But at this time Pope Alexander VI and King Ferdinand were not on the best of terms. When Alexander VI had become pope, he nominated his son Cesare Borgia as Archbishop of Valencia and Valdona. The Spanish Monarchs, however, had not given their consent to this nomination because Alexander VI's political views were hostile to Ferdinand of Aragon, King of Naples, and cousin of Ferdinand of Spain.

The Neapolitan Ferdinand was the son of Alfonso the Magnanimous, King of Aragon and Naples, who had divided his realm between his natural son Ferdinand, to whom he had given the Kingdom of Naples, and his brother Juan II, to whom he had given Aragon, Sicily and Sardinia. At the death of Juan II, Ferdinand 1st of Spain became King of Aragon and of the two Sicilies. Very strict family ties existed between the two Ferdinands.

Alexander VI had been elected pope thanks to the maneuvers of Ascanio Sforza, brother of Ludovico "Il Moro" Duke of Milan. The pope conducted a politics similar to the one of the Milanese duke in favor of Charles VIII, King of France, instead of the Spanish Monarchy's.

On May 22nd, 1492 Cardinal Ascanio wrote to his brother Ludovico: "... *Yesterday two letters arrived from Spain to our Lord which were announcing good things for our Holiness and, among others, the king and queen have demonstrated good intention toward our Holiness by allowing his son to receive the Archbishopric of Valencia and Valdona, because it was time to do things the way His Holiness wanted ...*" However, even in 1493, after Columbus' discovery, some hostilities still existed and the Spanish Kings reminded the papal ambassador "*.... The interfering in matters concerning His Grace was interfering in their own.*"

Amicable rapports between the Spanish Crown and the Pontiff were re-established after the marriage of the second son of Alexander VI, Giovanni Borgia Duke of Gandia, to the daughter of King Ferdinand's uncle, Maria Enriquez.

Alexander VI issued the Bull *"Inter Cetera"* (= among the rest) concerning the division of the new lands on May 3, 1493, which had to be annulled for a new *"Inter Cetera"* issued the day after and made public during the month of June. The third Bull *"Eximiae Devotionis"* (= of exceptional devotions) was made public in July 1493.

The first Bull had not clearly defined the demarcation line between the possessions of Spain and Portugal; therefore a second was needed to remedy the omissions of the first. The third finally resulted in uniting the spiritual privileges mentioned in the first and in limiting the demarcation line established in the second. The Bull *"Inter Cetera"* of May remains the most important because was defining *"La Raya"*—the line of demarcation between the possessions of Spain and the ones of Portugal one hundred leagues West of the Azores Islands tracing a straight route from the Arctic to the Antarctic Pole.

Alexander VI's Bulls confirm what Pope Nicholas V had already started in the one entitled *"Romanus Pontifex"* (=Roman Pontiff) of January 8, 1455 about the Portuguese colonization of Africa with the words: ... *"so that the barbaric populations be conquered and converted to Christianity ..."* charging in this manner Spain with the moral principal of evangelization.

The contents of Alexander VI's Bulls were based upon the information sent by the Spanish Monarchs as well as Columbus himself emphasizing the construction of *Fort Navidad* and the chosen men left there to continue the exploration and to convert the natives.

Portrait of Pope Alexander VI.
Courtesy of the Musée de Beaux Arts, Dijon.

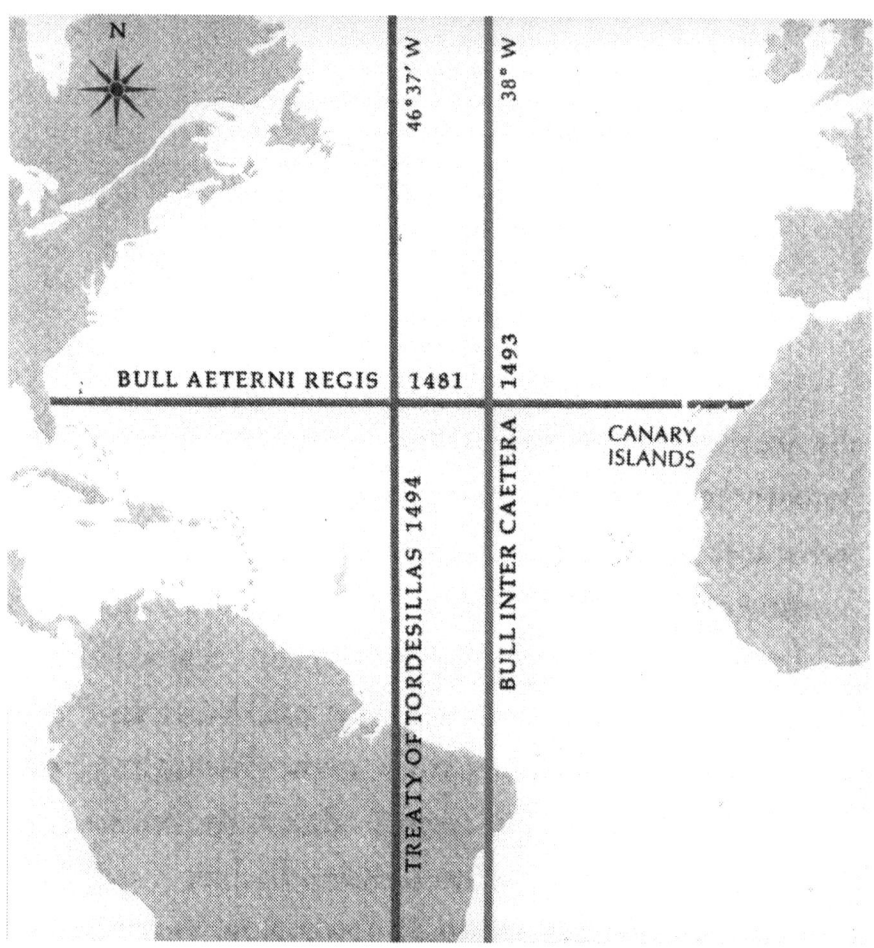

Demarcation lines according to Papal Bulls.
Panel at La Casa de Colón, Grand Canary.

Columbus' coat of arms at Municipal Palace, Genoa.

Columbus' coat of arms at House of Trade with the Indies,
Seville.

Columbus' coat of arms at La Rábida, Palos.

BIBLIOGRAPHY

Paolo Emilio Taviani: "*The Great Discovery.*" P. 127. Instituto Geografico de Agostini, Novara, Italy.

Synopsis

In 1992, during the festivities for the celebration of the Quincentenary of the discovery of America, Prof. Marinella Bonvini Mazzanti, Associate Professor of History at the University of Urbino, Italy, discovered, researching through documents written after Columbus' return from the first voyage, that there was a fourth ship accompanying the expedition.

At the time Senator Paolo Emilio Taviani was recognized all over the world as the authority on Columbian Studies and his books had been translated in many languages and shipped to schools and bookstores where the Quincentenary was celebrated.

Since the day Mrs. Rita Stark received Prof. Mazzanti's book, she had the idea of researching more about this fourth ship directly in Santo Domingo. On January 17, 18, and 19, 2004, while in Santo Domingo visiting the museum of the Royal Houses, the maritime Museum, and the House of Diego Colón she found the picture of this fourth ship used by the Portuguese during their raids, which originally was called "*Fusta.*"

The *Fusta* was a type of pirate ship used by the Portuguese during their raids along the African coast where there was no control and the Portuguese pirates could fill the cargo-hold with everything they could gather from their raids and sell for their own profits. It was a ship with very large cargo hold that could also carry quite a bit of weight, up to forty men, and withstand strong winds.

By the time Columbus was ready to sail the Ocean Sea many African and Mediterranean territories had become colonies under government regulations; so whoever wanted to continue piracy had to move their bases and Columbus' expedition would open new lands for such purpose as well as for legitimate business enterprises.

Apparently this "**fourth ship**" was not considered part of Columbus' expedition, but simply an extra caravel financed and equipped by private entrepreneurs, who simply wanted to follow him of their own free will.

When upon arrival to Española Columbus's flagship the "*Santa Maria*" was shipwrecked behind repair, *Fort Navidad* was built using all the lumber that could be salvaged from her. So it was conceivable that Columbus would leave the

Fusta for the 39 men left there to continue the exploration of the island while he returned to Spain on the *Niña* and the brothers Pinzón on the *Pinta*.

Chronology

3 August 1492: La Santa Maria, La Pinta, La Niña departed at dawn from the port of Palos.

12 August 1492: Arrival at Gomera in the Canary Islands.

6 September 1492: Departure from Gomera for Hierro.

8 September 1492: Departure from Hierro to begin the crossing of the Atlantic at 3 a.m.

11 October 1492: At about 10 p.m. Columbus sees a light.

12 October 1492: At 2 a.m. land is spotted and named San Salvador.

27 October 1492: At nightfall the island of Cuba is spotted.

6 December 1492: The ships reach the western point of the island of Española.

24-25 December 1492: During Christmas Eve Night the Santa Maria is shipwrecked. Columbus begins immediately the construction of Fort Navidad.

16 January 1493: At dawn La Pinta commanded by Martín Alonso Pinzón and La Niña commanded by Columbus begin the voyage of return.

4 March 1493: Columbus reaches the estuary of Tagus and proceeds to Lisbon.

15 March 1493: Columbus reaches the port of Palos around noon.

End of April 1493: The Spanish Monarchs receive the Admiral in Barcelona.

Monument in the garden of the Alcazar, Cordoba.

About the Author

Rita Marzochhi Stark is a naturalized American Citizen, who lived in this country for 40 years. Before coming to America in 1967, she was a teacher of History, Geography, and Art History in a Spanish Academy for girls in Montreux, Switzerland from 1959 to 1962 when she became a Public Accountant. She moved to Bern to work as an Accountant in a travel Agency where she was also guiding tours in Spain, France, Italy, and Germany because she could speak these languages.

In America she worked also as an Accountant until she retired and moved to St. Augustine Florida in 1990. In St. Augustine she met Prof. Vincente Paliotti, a retired Prof. of Economics who has taught at Northeastern University in Boston where she has taken an English course. He convinced her to take the English and Spanish courses required in this country to earn the equivalency to her Teaching Diploma and start writing books about her life experiences and European History that could help broaden the spectrum of knowledge in certain academic fields.

Between 2002 and 2006 she has written four books: *The Cliff of the Dragon and other European Legends* published by Xlibris, *Christmas Stories, The Pope's Daughter, Marie-Antoinette* published by iUniverse.

978-0-595-45702-1
0-595-45702-9

www.ingramcontent.com/pod-product-compliance
Lightning Source LLC
Chambersburg PA
CBHW051431280526
45785CB00003B/1243